BEACONSFIELD
AND BOLINGBROKE

Beaconsfield and Bolingbroke

by

RICHARD FABER

FABER AND FABER
24 Russell Square
London

*First published in mcmlxi
by Faber and Faber Limited
24 Russell Square London W.C.1
Printed in Great Britain by
Latimer Trend & Co Ltd Plymouth
All rights reserved*

© *Richard Faber* 1961

'. . . restoring the nation to its primitive temper and integrity, to its old good manners, its old good humor, and its old good nature (expressions of my lord chancellor Clarendon, which I could never read without being moved and softened). . . .'

BOLINGBROKE: *Dissertation upon Parties, Letter II*

'I now appeal to the House of Commons. . . . They may step in and do that which the Minister shrinks from doing—terminate the bitter controversy of years. They may bring back that which my Lord Clarendon called "the old good-nature of the people of England". . . .'

DISRAELI: *Speech on Agricultural Distress in 1851*

CONTENTS

9

ILLUSTRATIONS

PREFACE

I was attracted to a study of Disraeli as an under-
graduate, intrigued to discover a range of Tory
beliefs beyond the usual Conservative horizon.
Whatever his faults of falsity or exaggeration Disraeli's life and thought still have an odd power to fascinate,
at least young men. It is still possible, on reading *Coningsby*
for the first time, to feel a flicker of excitement that
made George Smythe exclaim: 'Thank God I have a
faith at last!' This is the more striking because Conservatism, except when it becomes a lost cause, is less apt to
excite than most political creeds. It seems to offer comparatively little scope for imagination or intellectual
acumen: there is a note of caution, of realism, sometimes
of self-interest, that may strike coldly on the romantic
mind. This is Disraeli's particular value to the Right
Wing: he helps the romantic to feel at home in a company that might otherwise seem rather hard-headed or
unenterprising for his taste.

If (as I suspect) Disraeli has more conversions to his
credit than any other British Conservative writer, his
political philosophy, whether or not outmoded or un-
real, is worth studying with something more than anti-

quarian zeal. Such a study soon shows that Disraeli was himself influenced as a young man in the same kind of way as he has since influenced others. To guess from his own acknowledgements it was Bolingbroke, more than any other single authority, who reconciled the young radical to membership of the Tory party. So the devout or curious student, anxious to pursue Disraeli's doctrine to its source, or perhaps to establish an 'apostolic succession' in Tory belief, turns eagerly to Bolingbroke's writings or career—and usually returns disillusioned. Bolingbroke has had his defenders; but it is more usual to admire only the style in his writings and to regard him personally as a brilliant charlatan. If so, in exalting Bolingbroke, Disraeli was simply creating a myth as he knew well how to do. Is that the whole truth of the matter? If it is, what did Bolingbroke in fact profess, and how and why did Disraeli magnify its importance? These are the questions that intrigued me when I first read Disraeli and that I try to answer in this essay.

This is not a piece of historical research. My subject is the political doctrine of Disraeli and Bolingbroke and only incidentally their characters or careers. Their characters of course help to explain their political beliefs and their careers may show how sincerely and effectively these were held. It is only with this in mind that I have made any study of their lives, which have attracted many, much better qualified writers. For Disraeli I have chiefly relied on the classic life by Monypenny and Buckle. (Murray: two-volume edition of 1929). Bolingbroke has never had such authoritative treatment: his character and achievements are both less widely known and more difficult to assess than those of Disraeli. For this reason, and particularly since his sincerity has so often been questioned,

I have prefaced my account of his opinions with a brief biographical sketch. This I owe mainly to the lives by Sichel (Nisbet, 2 volumes, 1901), Hassall (Blackwell, revised edition, 1915) and Petrie (Collins, 1937); also to a doctorate thesis by Paul Baratier (*Lord Bolingbroke. Ses écrits politiques.* Paris, 1939), which gives the best balanced verdict on Bolingbroke—except perhaps for Lord Chesterfield's contemporary *Character*—that I have read. Of general histories of the period, Feiling's *History of the Tory Party* (Oxford, 1924) is the most relevant to my theme. Among my few original sources I should mention Swift's Works (particularly the *Journal to Stella*) and Correspondence, and Parke's collection of Bolingbroke's correspondence during the years when he was Secretary of State, published in 1798.

My main business has been with the political writings of Bolingbroke and Disraeli themselves, two of the most articulate statesmen in British history. These of course have had their commentators too, who could not ignore Disraeli's debt, real or imaginary, to Bolingbroke. But I hope I am right in claiming that this debt has not been discussed so fully, or at least so exclusively, before. Apart from his speeches and letters (for which I have seldom looked further than the passages generously quoted by Monypenny and Buckle) Disraeli's political philosophy can be gathered from *The Vindication of the English Constitution* of 1835, which with other political writings is reproduced in *Whigs and Whiggism* edited by W. Hutcheon (Murray, 1913); from his *Political Biography of Lord George Bentinck*, first published in 1851; and from his novels *Coningsby, or the New Generation* (1844), *Sybil, or the Two Nations* (1845) and *Tancred, or the New Crusade* (1847). *Lothair* (1870) and *Endymion* (1880) are much less important; but Disraeli summarized his own early views more brilliantly than any critic has done in the General Preface to the Hughenden Edition of his novels, written in 1870. Bolingbroke's main political writings are *A Letter to Sir William Wyndham* (written in 1717, though not published till 1753); *Remarks on the History of England* and the *Dissertation upon Parties* (both originally contributed to *The Craftsman* between 1726 and 1734); *Letters on the Study and Use of History* (written in 1735–36); the *Letter on the Spirit of Patriotism* (written in 1736); *The Idea of a Patriot King* (written in 1738, revised 1745–47 and first authoritatively published in 1749); the dissertation *Of the State of Parties at the Accession of King George the First* and the unfinished *Some reflections on the present State of the Nation* (written in 1749). My references to these are from the first collected edition of Bolingbroke's works, published posthumously in 1754. I have not grappled seriously with his metaphysical writings, which shocked, dazzled or disgusted his contemporaries when they appeared after his death, but do not impress modern critics.*

I have planned and written this essay over a number of years, during odd moments of leisure, and with only occasional access to libraries. I hope this may partly explain why a slight, but I think attractive, theme has not been less slightly, and more attractively, developed.

* See, e.g. D. G. James' *The Life of Reason* (Longmans, Green and Co. 1949).

Chapter 1

DISRAELI

Disraeli survives in many images. The brilliant Jew who, in the face of all probability, became twice Prime Minister. The politician who was also a successful novelist. The extravagant young dandy. The witty but relentless opponent of Peel and Gladstone. The favourite Minister of Queen Victoria. The leader who prepared the Conservative Party for the Twentieth Century by putting it on a popular basis. The imperial statesman, who acquired Cyprus and control of the Suez Canal and who brought back 'peace with honour' from the Congress of Berlin.

Perhaps it is as the imperial statesman, the bearded Beaconsfield of Parliament Square, that Disraeli is most remembered. But this was almost his latest role. His efforts to strengthen and to popularize the Conservative Party (to reconcile progress with tradition and privilege with national unity) bulked much larger in his career as a whole. As a political thinker his most creative period was in his late thirties and early forties, before he had tasted power or responsibility, before he had found a secure place in the leadership of his party and well before the imperial projects of his later years.

B   17

Nobody disputes Disraeli's wit and courage. Nobody disputes the theatrical splendour of his career. Nobody disputes (even if they do not admire) his efforts to enlarge the Conservative Party and the British Empire. But there is a persistent tendency to regard him as a man without principle, to dismiss his concern with social reform as window-dressing and to set aside his political ideas as tawdry or insincere.

This is strange. From about the age of thirty Disraeli held his political views (in spite of fresh growths here and prunings there) with an articulateness and consistency unusual in politicians. In 1870, writing a General Preface to a new edition of his novels, he was still ready to stand publicly by the Trilogy of *Coningsby*, *Sybil* and *Tancred* which he had published a quarter of a century before. Echoes from his political novels sound continually in his speeches and letters. It would be wrong to suggest that these views were only for show and not for use. They bore fruit in various ways. Disraeli's attitude towards the Crown resulted—whether for good or ill—in his treatment of Queen Victoria and the effect it had on her. His sponsorship of the Second Reform Bill in 1867 may have been prompted by tactical advantage as much as by democratic conviction, though he had more than once suggested that 'the wider the popular suffrage the more powerful would be the natural aristocracy'.[1] But the 'sanitas sanitatum' theme of the Manchester Speech in 1872 and the social legislation of 1874–1878[2] were genuine results of his ambition to improve the condition of the people, of the concern that had led him to oppose the New Poor Law in 1837, on the grounds that relief to the poor was not a charity but a right. His imperialism, too, however it may be judged, certainly had its effect on affairs; although a late growth in his career, it can be traced to earlier seeds. This combined harvest of realized ideals is at least as much as most statesmen achieve.

It is true that Disraeli took time to develop his political outlook. In his twenties he hovered between the Whigs and Tories or despaired of both of them. He wanted a new 'national' party. It was not until 1835 that he dismissed this as a dream and proclaimed himself a Tory. But he had already advocated ideas (such as support for the clergy and improvement of working-class conditions) that he was to hold throughout his life. At the end of 1835 he published his *Vindication of the English Constitution*. Although the *Vindication* was largely written as propaganda on behalf of the House of Lords, and although it is less monarchical and more liberty-loving in tone than the political novels of the next decade, the four main facets of Disraeli's mature Toryism are, to a large extent, already implicit in it:

(*a*) Opposition to abstract ideas in politics. (Disraeli's first political essay, *The Voyage of Captain Popanilla* published in 1828, had been a skit on Benthamism, which he never ceased to detest; Whig dependence on abstract 'cosmopolitan' principles was one of the reasons why, although he found the Whigs more cultivated and amusing than the Tories, he never joined them.)

(*b*) Support for the landed interest, conceived as the backbone of the nation. (Years later, in 1880, Disraeli wrote in a letter to Lord Salisbury: 'During a long parliamentary life, and long before I was in Parliament, I have been profoundly convinced that the greatness and character of this country depended on our landed tenure. All the rest I look upon, and have ever looked upon, as leather and prunella'. He was fond of saying that it was this landed tenure that had pulled the country through the Napoleonic wars. 'Property has its duties as well as its rights', or, 'the tenure of property should be the fulfilment of duty', was a favourite theme of his and one more easily applied to landed than to other forms of property.)

(c) Reverence for existing, and sometimes for desuete, institutions. (Disraeli was later to lay special emphasis on the potential power and value of the Crown. He always supported the established church, though he gradually ceased to look on it as the 'Estate of the People' and, after the secession of Newman, began to doubt its ability to renovate the national spirit. His references to Parliament were not always complimentary—it was Tancred who spoke of 'that fatal drollery called a representative government.'—but became more so as he succeeded there; he at no time proposed, though he half-prophesied in *Coningsby*, a decrease in its powers.)

(d) Concern for the welfare of the people. (This is not in fact a dominant theme of the *Vindication*, which is not concerned with social or economic questions, although it does commend 'the equality that elevates and creates', the principle that 'everyone should be privileged' and the opportunities in England for progress within the social order. But *Sybil* is almost exclusively devoted to the living conditions of the working classes.)

These principles could stand as the four main pillars of Disraeli's political thought throughout his career. (There is more to say later of the fire burning within the temple.) Some more or less temporary wreaths were hung on them at the time of the 'Young England' movement, when the Trilogy of political novels was published. At that time Disraeli found himself at the head of a group of ardent young Tories, notably George Smythe and Lord

John Manners, who were under the influence of the tractarian movement. 'Young England' was romantically attached to the medieval church and to the early Stuart monarchy, distressed by the separation of classes and the sufferings of the poor, hostile to the commercial middle class and anxious to revive the customs and amenities of Merry England. A lot of harsh things have been said about 'Young England' (Morley wrote of its 'childish bathos') but its revolt against the drab industrial morality of the age was genuine enough. Its aspirations were glitteringly displayed, with a wealth of fiction and history, or at least historico-fiction, in *Coningsby* and *Sybil*. In these works, both influencing and influenced by his supporters, Disraeli proposed a revival of Crown and Church influence with the object of restoring national spirit and unity and securing an improvement in the lot of the poor.

Disraeli was careful not to get too deeply involved in 'Young England'. After canvassing his constituents in August 1844 he wrote to his wife that he found them 'a little alarmed in some quarters about Popery, monasteries and John Manners. This I shall quietly soften down.' His references to the movement in *Tancred* (dedicated to the 'Great Asian Mystery' of race and religion) were more detached than in the two earlier novels of the Trilogy; he later wrote that, by the time *Tancred* appeared, 'the Young England myth had evaporated'; when he looked back on the movement in *Endymion* (1880) he did not hide its more comic side. But he never repudiated his association with it and treated it handsomely in the General Preface to the Novels, written in 1870.

No doubt 'Young England' should not be taken too seriously. But it was the judgement of an anonymous biographer of Lord John Manners in 1872[3] that, although the movement's proposals were vague and perhaps impracticable, it 'did much to improve the moral atmosphere, and to dissipate the dogged bigotry and selfish materialism of Modern England.' Influences of this kind may of course be important, even if it is difficult to identify concrete results; this would indeed be true of much of Disraeli's teaching.

It is worth insisting that Disraeli expressed his political views frequently, completely, frankly and—on the whole —consistently. It was not always to his political advantage that he should do so. His career cannot have been helped, for instance, by his continual references to the virtues of the Jewish race. The charges of insincerity so often brought against him do not survive an effort to understand his writings and career. But why these charges occur is not difficult to understand. Disraeli's mind was complex, at once romantic and ironical; it came naturally to him to mock and admire at the same time. Although his ambition was profound, he could describe himself when he first became Prime Minister as having 'climbed to the top of the greasy pole.' The flamboyant and mysterious style which he loved to adopt in his more poetic passages was not likely to inspire the plain man with confidence. Nor was his skill at flattery or his tendency to disguise his personal feelings: habits derived from his racial background or learned in his long climb to power. Perhaps there were also more solid reasons for mistrust. Disraeli's principles were not always to the fore during the political manœuvres of his middle period. He was always ready to be flexible, but in the 50s and 60s he sometimes carried this flexibility to rather surprising lengths. (His private approach to Bright in 1852 when he had in mind a possible coalition with Bright and Cobden, is an example.) At least it must have seemed so to some of his aristocratic supporters or to some of his high-minded opponents. But then Disraeli had no family on which to rely; no interest with which to identify himself; no ready-made political beliefs; nothing but his own talents to bring him—in what must often have seemed an unconscionable time—to power. His views were his own and, in a sense, he was free to do what he liked with them. As he himself claimed in 1846: 'I am not in a condition to have had hereditary opinions carved out for me and all my opinions, therefore, have been the result of reading and thought.' There is no evidence that Disraeli would have jettisoned an essential part of his political beliefs to secure a tactical advantage; but he had certainly learned the need to suppress or suspend or to discard frills.

Fundamentally it is impossible to understand Disraeli in terms of the middle or late Victorian periods. He grew up with the Romantic Movement. His temperament was naturally in tune with it and his education and foreign travels fed the romantic vein. His political opinions were opposed to those of Byron, but he was none the less a distinctly Byronic figure. He had all the romantic's love of spectacular and colourful action, combined with intense feeling and restless thought; above all he had the romantic's faith in the almost limitless possibilities of individual achievement. His romanticism naturally became more sedate as he grew older; it turned more easily into cynicism; but it never disappeared. The disillusioned old man, pausing to digest between each course at Hughenden, still had his peacocks strutting and screaming on the terrace.

It is this attitude to life that explains the fascination that power had for Disraeli and his determination to acquire it. He was a man of ideas; but, in the last resort, character mattered more to him. What seized his imagination most was the influence of character (whether of the individual or the race) on history. It was certainly his own ambition to influence history, and he realized increasingly, as time went on, that the greatest impact was to be made in foreign, or imperial, affairs. Hence the pre-occupations of his later years. 'Real politics are the possession and distribution of power. I want to see you give your mind to foreign affairs . . .' says a character in his last novel *Endymion*. In a speech in the House of Commons in 1863 he outlined what the principles of his external policy would be: 'The statesmen who construct, and the warriors who achieve, are only influenced by the instinct of power, and animated by the love of country. Those are the feelings and those the methods which form empires.' There was nothing cosmopolitan in Disraeli's attitude towards external affairs; general principles, other than the interests of his country, had no place in it. But he was able to claim (at Manchester in 1872) that he was not 'of that school of statesmen who are favourable to a turbulent and aggressive diplomacy,' and that he had 'resisted it during a great part of my life.'

A statesman identifies his own ambition with that of his country. Disraeli wished personally to influence affairs; it seemed to him proper that his country, or his adopted race, should do so too. That was, in brief, the motive of his imperialism. '. . . in external affairs' he told the electors of Buckinghamshire on his elevation to the peerage in 1876, 'I have endeavoured to develop and strengthen our Empire, believing that combination of achievement and responsibility elevates the character and condition of a people.'

Portrait of Disraeli, at Hughenden,
by Sir Francis Grant, 1852
(*see overleaf*)

Benjamin Disraeli
1804–1881
First elected to Parliament, 1837
Opposed Peel's repeal of the Corn Laws, 1846
Leader of the Tory Party in the House of
Commons, 1849–1876
Chancellor of the Exchequer, 1852, 1858–1859
and 1866–1868
Carried Second Reform Bill in the Commons, 1867
Prime Minister, 1868 and 1874–1880
Created Earl of Beaconsfield, 1876
Principal British negotiator at the
Congress of Berlin, 1878.

He was intensely conscious and proud of his Jewish blood. Although an Anglican in religion he never ceased to believe that the Jews were, in a sense, a chosen people. Other peoples, or races, certainly had their seasons too. The Anglo-Saxons were having their day in the Nineteenth Century; they had stamped their 'diligent and methodic character on the century.'[4] In Africa they were superior to the Negro populations and, as such, were right not to mix with them and thus risk deterioration and absorption.[5] But other races might come along later, with improved methods and ideals, and assert a new ascendancy. The Jews had the advantage, only shared with the inhabitants of the pure Arabian desert, of being 'an unmixed race'; as long as they remained so they were sure of a basic and permanent superiority over all mixed races, since 'an unmixed race of a first-rate organization are the aristocracy of Nature.'[6]

Disraeli's views on race had a profound effect on his thought from the time of the Trilogy onwards. His discovery that the principle of race was 'the key of history' was announced by Sidonia in the Trilogy ('all is race, there is no other truth. . . .') and confirmed by Baron Sergius in *Endymion*. It would be interesting to know what prompted him to this line of thought. Sidonia— unlike Baron Sergius—could not possibly have read de Gobineau's famous *Essay on the Inequality of Human Races*, which was not published until the 1850s. But he might almost have subscribed to de Gobineau's words: 'Gradually I have become convinced that race overshadows all other problems in history, that it holds the key to them all and that the inequality of races from whose fusion a people is formed is enough to explain the whole course of its destiny'.

The physiological basis of Disraeli's racial theory, with its belief in the inherent superiority of one race over another and in the virtue of unmixed stock, has of course been discredited since. Disraeli got into difficulties with it himself, which might have revealed its absurdity. Writing to Lord Derby in 1861 he described Louis Napoleon as 'head of the Latin race'; but, by the time of *Endymion*, Baron Sergius had concluded that the Latin race did not exist. After the excesses of Nazism the doctrine has ugly associations, particularly when it is coupled with Disraeli's imperialism and his tendency to sympathize with absolute government. (Thus he said to Vitzthum, after the death of the Prince Consort, for whom he had a great admiration: 'If he had outlived some of our "old stagers" he would have given us, while retaining all constitutional guarantees, the blessings of absolute government.') It may be a tribute to Disraeli's prescience that he realized so early the force of ideas that were to result in Nazi totalitarianism; but his partisans would not wish to emphasize this side of his thought today.

Yet there is this much to be said. Disraeli's absolutism was traditional, not revolutionary; his imperialism was conceived in technicolor, not in an aggressive black and white. India was a jewel in the Queen's crown, not the Empire's milch-cow. There was no intolerance in his outlook and he certainly never spoke, or wrote, in favour of violent change. If he contemplated an increase in the power of the Crown it was largely because the Crown had traditionally enjoyed such power. He never wanted traditional liberties, as he understood them, to be suppressed. He frequently attacked the evils of excessive centralization; he visualized (in *Coningsby*) a 'free monarchy, established on fundamental laws, itself the apex of a vast pile of municipal and local government, ruling an educated people, represented by a free and intellectual press.' *Imperium et libertas* was, in short, his motto. It was from the theocratic traditions of Judaism that his monarchical bias derived. He knew that the 'Anglo-Saxon race' had other traditions exalting personal freedom; he admired these too and never proposed to violate them.

Nor were Disraeli's views on race as sinister as the foregoing might suggest. The racist evils of this century have hardly been caused by belief in the superiority of the Jewish race. If Disraeli regarded the white colonists in Africa as intrinsically superior to the Negroes, that was a common enough assumption at the time. Unmixed races apart, he does not seem to have believed firmly in the invariable or lasting superiority of one race over another.[7] It is true that he regarded history as a kind of struggle between races and assumed that a vigorous race would seek to expand its civilization. But that is not yet an outmoded point of view, even if the political or military conquest of weaker countries—as opposed to their economic or cultural penetration—is no longer in fashion.

As well as being less sinister, Disraeli's racial doctrine may be less silly than it seems at first sight. It is not necessarily worthless because some of its assumptions are scientifically unsound. There may be no 'unmixed' races; it may be historical or physiological nonsense that 'a superior race shall never be destroyed or absorbed by an inferior.' But when Disraeli makes Sidonia say 'all is race, there is no other truth' he is not only talking biology. The oracle was meant to be taken literally. Other passages in his writings confirm that it was really his view that each race (or people) evolved its own customs and ideals to suit its own genius and would only achieve success by remaining true to them and eschewing imitation.[8] This view does not depend upon, although it may find support in, a belief in the value of racial purity.

'All is race, there is no other truth'. Disraeli seems in fact to have come to regard all religious, artistic and philosophic principles as reflections of national genius, without any universal validity. There was perhaps one exception in his mind: the divine truths entrusted to the specially favoured—and unmixed—Semitic race; he seems to have thought that these were intended by providence for retail to other peoples. Perhaps it is not of great importance to enquire exactly how much these truths meant personally to Disraeli. As far as I know, he never queried them. But then he was not basically a religious man. Or at least he found no difficulty in devoting his religion to political ends. He held that government should be divine, in the sense that it should command and satisfy loyalty and faith. But he usually spoke of organized religion as if it were an instrument in achieving national purpose. His identification of religious with political government was peculiarly Hebraic.

Seen in this light Disraeli's racial doctrine no longer appears a vulgar excrescence on his political thought, but an essential part of it. It helps to justify his Toryism and his regard for the national past. It provides a natural setting for the four guiding ideas listed earlier in this chapter. At the same time (and the conclusion is suitably Disraelian) it subordinates these and other ideas to the development of national character.

Chapter 2

DISRAELI AND BOLINGBROKE

'In the early part of the last century, the Tory party required a similar reorganization to that which it has lately undergone; and as it is in the nature of human affairs that the individual that is required shall not long be wanting, so in the season of which I am treating arose a man remarkable in an illustrious age, who, with the splendour of an organizing genius, settled the confused and discordant materials of English faction, and reduced them into a clear and systematic order. This was Lord Bolingbroke. . . .'

'Gifted with that fiery imagination, the teeming fertility of whose inventive resources is as necessary to a great statesman or a great general as to a great poet; the ablest writer and the most accomplished orator of his age, that rare union that in a country of free Parliaments and a free press insures to its possessor the privilege of exercising a constant influence over the mind of his country, that rare union that has rendered Burke so memorable; blending with that intuitive knowledge of his race, which creative minds alone enjoy, all the wisdom which can be derived from literature and a comprehensive experience of human affairs—no one was better qualified to be the Minister of a free and powerful nation than Henry St. John; and Destiny at first appeared to combine with Nature in the elevation of his fortunes. Opposed to the Whigs from principle, for an oligarchy is hostile to genius, and recoiling from the Tory tenets, which his unprejudiced and vigorous mind taught him at the same time to dread and to condemn, Lord Bolingbroke, at the outset of his career, incurred the common-place imputation of insincerity and inconsistency, because, in an age of unsettled parties with professions contradictory of their conduct, he maintained that vigilant and meditative independence which is the privilege of an original and determined spirit. It is probable that in the earlier years of his career he meditated over the formation of a new party, that dream of youthful ambition in a perplexed and discordant age, but destined in English politics to be never more substantial than a vision. More experienced in political life, he became aware that he had only to choose between the Whigs and the Tories, and his sagacious intellect, not satisfied with the superficial character of these celebrated divisions penetrated their interior and essential qualities and discovered, in spite of all the affectation of popular sympathy on one side, and of admiration of arbitrary power on the other, that this choice was in fact a choice between oligarchy and democracy. From the moment that Lord Bolingbroke, in becoming a Tory, embraced the national cause, he devoted himself absolutely to his party: all the energies of his Protean mind were lavished in their service; and although the ignoble prudence of the Whig Minister restrained him from advocating the cause of the nation in the senate, it was his inspiring pen that made Walpole tremble in the recesses

of the Treasury, and in a series of writings, unequalled in
our literature for their spirited patriotism, their just and
profound views, and the golden eloquence in which they
are expressed, eradicated from Toryism all those absurd
and odious doctrines which Toryism had adventitiously
adopted, clearly developed its essential and permanent
character, discarded *jure divino*, demolished passive
obedience, threw to the winds the doctrine of non-
resistance, placed the abolition of James and the accession
of George on their right basis, and in the complete
reorganization of the public mind laid the foundation for
the future accession of the Tory party to power, and to
that popular and triumphant career which must ever
await the policy of an administration inspired by the
spirit of our free and ancient institutions.'

These lavish tributes are from Chapters 30 and 31 of
the *Vindication*. They are the fullest, but not the first, of
Disraeli's references to Bolingbroke. Three years earlier,
speaking to supporters at High Wycombe, he had
touched on the principles of primitive Toryism, advocated a return to triennial parliaments and described
'my Lord Bolingbroke' (also an advocate of triennial
parliaments in opposition) as 'one of the ablest men who
ever lived.' His interest in Bolingbroke seems to go back
even earlier. Disraeli's first novel *Vivian Grey* (written
when he was rising 21) has the following passage:

'Mr. Vivian Grey proceeded with the utmost sang-
froid; he commented upon expressions, split and subtil-
ized words, insinuated opinions, and finally quoted a
whole passage of Bolingbroke to prove that the opinion
of the most noble the Marquess of Carabas was one of the

soundest, wisest and most convincing of opinions that ever was promulgated by mortal man . . . [the passage was, in Vivian Grey's way, fictitious] . . . when the buzz had somewhat subsided, Mr. Grey looked smiling to his son, and said, "Vivian, my dear, can you tell me in what work of Bolingbroke I can find the eloquent passage you have just quoted?" "Ask Mr. Hargraves, sir" replied the son, with perfect coolness; then, turning to the member, "You know, Mr. Hargraves, you are reputed the most profound political student in the House, and more intimately acquainted than any other person with the works of Bolingbroke." '

The quotations from the *Vindication* do not tell us much about Bolingbroke's political views, except that he had a 'national' outlook and got rid of a lot of dead wood in Tory doctrine. Some passages in *Sybil* are more explicit. Bolingbroke is there again portrayed as having 'restored the moral existence' of the Tory party and as having 'taught them to recur to the ancient principles of their connection. . . .' After his death, his mantle is shown to have fallen on Lord Shelburne and later—during his earlier and happier years—on the younger Pitt. 'When the fine genius of the injured Bolingbroke, the only peer of his period who was educated, and proscribed by the oligarchy because they were afraid of his eloquence, "the glory of his order and the shame," shut out from Parliament, found vent in those writings which recalled to the English people the inherent blessings of their old free monarchy, and painted in immortal hues his picture of a patriot king, the spirit that he raised at length touched the heart of Carteret. . . .'

So Bolingbroke laid his hands on Carteret, who in turn laid his on his son-in-law, Shelburne. Lord Shelburne 'adopted from the first the Bolingbroke system; a real royalty in lieu of a chief magistracy; a permanent alliance with France, instead of the Whig scheme of viewing in that power the natural enemy of England; and, above all, a plan of commercial freedom, the germ of which may be found in the long-maligned negotiation of Utrecht, but which, in the instance of Lord Shelburne, was soon in time matured by all the economical science of Europe, in which he was a proficient.'

In due course Lord Shelburne laid his hands on Pitt. But, alas, not long enough, since the revolutionary age forced Pitt into reactionary courses and the Tory 'apostolic succession' temporarily lapsed. Nevertheless the verdict stands: 'Venetian politics, Dutch finance and French wars: against which, in their happier days, and with their happiest powers, struggled the three greatest of English statesmen—Bolingbroke, Shelburne and, lastly, the son of Chatham.' (In the first, unhallowed, trinity, 'Venetian politics' stands for the rule of an oligarchy, with a doge substituted for a sovereign; 'Dutch finance'—Dutch because introduced under William III—seems to refer to the national debt with the consequent 'degradation of a fettered and burthened multitude' and, more generally, to the deification of a financial Mammon; 'French wars', of course, means wars with France.)

After the Trilogy there are fewer references to Bolingbroke in Disraeli's speeches and writings. But we find him writing to his young protégé, Lord Henry Lennox, in 1856: 'With respect to our alliance with France generally, my opinions are upon record; in detail, even so late as 1853. I inherited them from Lord Bolingbroke, and the changes in the world, subsequent to his time, only confirm his prescience.' Disraeli was now fifty; old enough to have got over the youthful enthusiasm of the *Vindication* (though he was not so very youthful then) had it been no more than that. If he regarded a 'permanent alliance with France' as one of the three props of 'the Bolingbroke system', he saw 'a plan of commercial freedom' as another. Here again we find him as late as 1870 (in the General Preface to the Novels) referring to Bolingbroke's commercial principles at Utrecht as being 'subsequently and triumphantly vindicated by his pupil and heir, Mr. Pitt.' And in 1867, in a speech at an Edinburgh banquet, he was still referring to Bolingbroke and his supporters, while vindicating the Tories' historic title to deal with internal political reform.

From these references we can gather that Bolingbroke's main contributions to English political thought were, according to Disraeli:

(*a*) he gave Toryism a spring clean, helped it out of the intricacies of divine right and non-resistance and so paved the way for its return to power;

(*b*) he brought out the popular side of Toryism and supported triennial parliaments in an effort to prevent a growth of oligarchic control;

(*c*) he recalled the virtues of the old, free, English monarchy and wished the throne to be strengthened against the oligarchy;

(*d*) he favoured a measure of free trading with the continent;

(*e*) he advocated a permanent alliance with France.

The attraction for Disraeli of the first three of these attitudes is obvious. As to the fourth, support not for the dogma, but for concrete measures, of free trade must have seemed a good cry: at once progressive, enlightened and realistic. If it could be represented as genuinely and traditionally Tory (for the Tory, like the Common Law, prefers to build on precedent) the party might escape some of the odium arising from its reluctance to abandon protection for the landed interest. As to the fifth it is difficult to see anything specifically or necessarily Tory in support for an Anglo-French alliance. Here it seems conceivable that Disraeli, who in 1830 had written a hostile tract on *Gallomania*, later became a francophile more or less in imitation of Bolingbroke. At least that is what his letter to Lord Henry Lennox might suggest; and his hostility to 'French wars' smacks rather of Marlborough's campaigns than of the fight against Napoleon. However this may be, he spent some time in Paris in the early 1840s, saw something of Louis Philippe and seems to have hoped for help (presumably financial as well as moral) in building up a pro-French party in England.

Doctrine apart, Disraeli must have been attracted by Bolingbroke's dash, style and personality. St. John's youth on entering politics, the unsteady brilliance of his reputation, his thirst for pleasure and experience, his power of expression, his looks and eloquence: all these qualities were Byronic enough to fascinate the young Disraeli.[1] He must have felt what separated him from the aristocrat who, while still in his twenties, found the world of politics at his feet. But he shared with Bolingbroke unusual political and literary gifts; the two men also had in common fluent imagination, belief in individual genius and intense ambition.

Disraeli's references to Bolingbroke in 1832 and in the *Vindication* suggest that his hero was much in his mind when he decided to join the Tory Party. In the second of the quotations from the *Vindication* at the head of this chapter, the whole of the passage which begins 'Opposed to the Whigs from principle . . .' and ends '. . . this choice was in fact a choice between oligarchy and democracy' is almost blatantly autobiographical in its aptness to Disraeli himself. This was not lost on at any rate one contemporary. Writing to his sister at the beginning of 1836 Disraeli quoted from a letter he had had from Lord Eliot: 'He says, among other things, "In reading your sketch of Bolingbroke I could not help thinking that if opportunities are not withheld you may become what he might have been" '.

Whether or not Disraeli ever became what Bolingbroke might have been there were moments in his career when his position must have reminded him of his predecessor's. When he was associated with Lord George Bentinck in opposition to Peel did he see himself as Lord George's mentor, as Bolingbroke had been Sir William Wyndham's? He certainly thought of his friends as a 'country party', like the one of which Sir William had been a 'natural leader'. When he acquired the Hughenden estate did he have in mind Bolingbroke's country pursuits at Bucklebury and Dawley? When he was associated with Young England did he recall Bolingbroke's connection with the 'Boy Patriots' in his old age? At any rate the end of *Sybil*:

'That we may live to see England once more possess a free Monarchy and a privileged and prosperous People, is my prayer; that these great consequences can only be brought about by the energy and devotion of our youth is my persuasion. We live in an Age when to be young and to be indifferent can no longer be synonymous. We must prepare for the coming hour. The claims of the Future are represented by suffering millions; and the youth of a Nation are the trustees of Posterity.'

is, *mutatis mutandis*, reminiscent of Bolingbroke's *Letter on the Spirit of Patriotism*:

'I expect little from the principal actors that tread the stage at present . . . I turn my eyes from the generation that is going off, to the generation that is coming on the stage. I expect good from them. . . .'

But a more lasting parallel was Disraeli's lifelong work of reconstructing the Tory party and of saving it (as Bolingbroke had saved it from the Jacobites) from its Old Guard. He wrote in a letter in 1874: 'I have, for forty years, been labouring to replace the Tory party in their natural and historical position in the country. I am in the sunset of life, but I do not despair of seeing my purpose effected.'

He was then about to enter on his last Ministry. He was to establish an ascendency over his sovereign firmer than Bolingbroke's in the last months of Queen Anne. At last, in his seventies, he was to take part in international negotiations as Bolingbroke had in his thirties; he would have the Congress of Berlin to set alongside the Treaty of Utrecht. This was still in the future. But he could already compare himself with the man who, in his own words, 'laid the foundation for the future accession of the Tory party to power.'

A fork once belonging to Bolingbroke is displayed in the 'Disraeli Room' at Hughenden, next to a lock of Byron's hair. The one coloured Disraeli's political imagination, as the other his ideal.

Chapter 3

BOLINGBROKE

'I think Mr. St. John the greatest young man I ever knew; wit, capacity, beauty, quickness of apprehension, good learning and an excellent taste; the best orator in the House of Commons, admirable conversation, good nature and good manners; generous and a despiser of money. His only fault is talking to his friends in way of complaint of too great a load of business, which looks a little like affectation; and he endeavours too much to mix the fine gentleman, and man of pleasure, with the man of business. What truth and sincerity he may have I know not: he is now but thirty-two, and has been Secretary above a year.'

SWIFT: *Journal to Stella*, 1711

'My Lord Bolingbroke was of a nature frank and open; and, as men of great genius are superior to common rules, he seldom gave himself the trouble of disguising or sobering his resentments, although he was ready enough to forget them. In matters of state, as the earl [of Oxford: Harley] was too reserved, so, perhaps, the other was too free; not from any incontinency of talk, but from the mere contempt of multiplying secrets; although the graver counsellors imputed this liberty of speech to vanity or lightness.'

. . . what I have often wondered at in a man of his temper, was his prodigious application, whenever he thought it necessary; for he would plod whole days and nights, like the lowest clerk in an office.'

> SWIFT: *Enquiry into the behaviour of the Queen's last Ministry*, 1715

'Il me dit, que je sçavois bien, par son caractère, qu'il ne faisoit pas les choses à demi. . . .'

> LORD STAIR, H.M. Ambassador in Paris: letter to Mr. James Craggs

'J'ai trouvé dans cet illustre Anglais toute l'érudition de son pays et toute la politesse du nôtre.'

> VOLTAIRE, 1722

'Let us suppose, in this, or some other unfortunate country, an anti-Minister, who thinks himself a person of so great and extensive parts, and of so many eminent qualifications, that he looks upon himself as the only person in the kingdom capable to conduct the public affairs of the nation . . . we may suppose this leader not really liked by any, even of those who so blindly follow him, and hated by all the rest of mankind . . . void of all faith and honour, and betraying every master he ever served . . . can there be imagined a greater disgrace to human nature than such a wretch as this.'

> WALPOLE: speech during Commons debate on the repeal of the Septennial Act, 1734

'I have lately seen some writings of Lord Bolingbroke's, since he went to France. Nothing can depress his genius. Whatever befalls him, he will still be the greatest man in the world, either in his own time, or with posterity.'

POPE: letter to Swift, 1736

'He had, it is true, his faults, which proceeded from unbounded ambition and impetuous passions; but they have now subsided to age and experience; and I can wish you nothing better than to be what he is now, without being what he has been formerly.'

CHESTERFIELD: to his son, 1749

'Lord Bolingbroke joined all the politeness, the manners and the graces of a courtier, to the solidity of a statesman and to the learning of a pedant. He was *omnis homo*. . . .'

CHESTERFIELD: to his son, 1752

'He had noble and generous sentiments, rather than fixed, reflected principles of good-nature and friendship; but they were more violent than lasting, and suddenly and often varied to their opposite extremes, with regard even to the same person.'

From CHESTERFIELD's *Characters*

'. . . the least trifle, such as the over-roasting of a leg of mutton, would strangely disturb and ruffle his temper . . . his passions constantly got the better of his judgement . . . no man was more partial to his friends and more ready to oblige them . . . but . . . he was a most bitter enemy to those he hated. . . .'

> CHESTERFIELD: in a private
> conversation recorded by his
> biographer, Dr. Maty

'Pitt told me coolly, that he had read this book formerly, when he admired Lord Bolingbroke more than he does now.'

> HORACE WALPOLE: letter to
> H. Mann, 1749

'inimitable beauty of the style, as well as the matter. . . .'

> PITT: on Bolingbroke's
> *Remarks on the History of
> England*, to his nephew, 1754

'Lord Bolingbroke was of a temper to overturn kingdoms to make way for himself and his talents to govern the world.'

> Verdict of Bolingbroke's
> contemporary, SPEAKER ONSLOW

'Sir, he was a scoundrel, and a coward; a scoundrel, for charging a blunderbuss against religion and morality; a coward, because he had not resolution to fire it off himself, but left half a crown to a beggarly Scotchman, to draw the trigger after his death.'

> DR. JOHNSON on the posthumous
> publication of Lord Bolingbroke's
> philosophical works, 1754

'. . . a man of warm imagination and elegant taste,

penetrating, eloquent, ambitious and enterprising, whose talents were rather specious than solid, and whose principles were loose and fluctuating. . . .'

SMOLLETT: *History of England, c.* 1762

'I do not often quote Bolingbroke, nor have his works in general left any permanent impression on my mind. He is a presumptious and a superficial writer. But he has one observation, which, in my opinion, is not without depth and solidity. He says, that he prefers a monarchy to other governments; because you can better ingraft any description of republic on a monarchy than anything of monarchy upon the republican forms. I think him perfectly in the right. The fact is so historically; and it agrees well with the speculation.'

BURKE: *Reflections on the Revolution in France,* 1790

'His lordship's philosophy, such as it was, was the newest pattern of the day, and of course excited considerable notice, as coming from a man who had made a conspicuous figure in politics; and whose career, after a youth spent in the stews, and a manhood in turbulence and disaffection to the government of his country, seemed appropriately terminated by an old age of infidelity.'

JAMES PRIOR: *Life of Burke,* 1824

'We are indeed no admirers of the statesmen who concluded that peace. Harley, we believe, was a solemn trifler, St. John a brilliant knave . . . But, on the great question of Peace or War, we cannot but think that, although their motives may have been selfish and

malevolent, their decision was beneficial to the state.'
                    MACAULAY: *Essay on the War*
                    of succession in Spain, 1833

'In every part he was a consummate posture-master . . .
of all the characters in our history, Bolingbroke must be
pronounced to be most of a charlatan; of all the writing in
our literature, his is the hollowest, the flashiest, the most
insincere.'
                    MORLEY: *Life of Walpole*, 1889

'We think of him as the brilliant orator, the almost
unrivalled parliamentary debater, the great prose writer,
the fascinating man of fashion, the reckless libertine, the
versatile political conspirator . . . a man of genius and,
intellectually at least the greatest English statesman of his
time . . . a certain lack of sincerity in politics as well as in
thought prevented him from rendering at any time full
justice to his own intellectual capabilities. As a statesman
he seems to have been absolutely without any guiding
principle, and his efforts to be a great thinker brought him
to no higher place than that of a brilliant but an easy
sceptic . . . (Bolingbroke) seemed to regard the whole
course of living history merely as a path for him to tread
towards the satisfaction of his own personal ambition.'
                    J. McCARTHY: *Reign of Queen Anne*, 1902

'. . . in the main he succeeded in imposing England's
will on Europe. And in so doing he gave the world a
peace that proved more suited to the needs of the new
century than the post-Napoleonic treaties of Vienna, or
the Versailles Treaty of our own day.'
                    TREVELYAN: *England under Queen Anne*, 1934

43

'. . . perhaps no great man ever needed the sympathy of imagination leavening judgement more than Henry St. John, the first Viscount Bolingbroke.'

SICHEL: *Bolingbroke and his Times*, 1901

' 'tis no matter what the world says of us. If a man is sensible that he has always acted for the good of his country, he may always lay down his head with pleasure on his pillow. . . .'

BOLINGBROKE: 1744

These quotations show how variously, and how emphatically, Bolingbroke has been judged. If they agree at all it is only in suggesting that he was not dull. In his lifetime Bolingbroke was regarded with admiration and distrust; after his death the admiration waned and the distrust grew. Posterity tended to regard his youthful dissipations and his mercurial career more severely than his contemporaries. But perhaps his reputation suffered most from the posthumous publication of his free-thinking writings on religion. Nineteenth-century historians could accuse him of a triple lack of moral, political and religious principle. Twentieth-century historians, though less shocked by his private life and religious beliefs, have found it difficult to discover a consistent pattern in his political conduct or any real depth and solidity in his political writings. His few warm supporters, reacting violently to violent attacks, have only partly rehabilitated him. His skill in negotiating the treaty of Utrecht is allowed, though his methods questioned; otherwise almost his only undisputed excellence is as an orator—dead laurels, since none of his speeches survive.

In all, he appears as a minor and tarnished Alcibiades; his youthful brilliance obscured, without his respectability being enhanced, by a petulant old age and the row of pompous looking volumes that contain his works.

Complex people need complicated judgements. Bolingbroke was sometimes known to his friends as 'Mercurialis'. Chesterfield wrote of the strong lights and shades in his character.[1] His critics have tended to underrate his complexity and to dismiss him as empty, scheming, or insincere.

Bolingbroke's private life was colourful, but comparatively straightforward. Born of an aristocratic family he had ancestors on both sides in the Civil Wars. His father was a rake; his mother died when he was a boy, leaving him to be brought up by his pious, low-church, grandparents in Battersea Manor House. After going to Eton he spent nearly two years on the continent, where he learned fluent French and Italian. When he was twenty-two he made a good, but on his side apparently loveless, match and was not a model husband. After his wife's early death—his flight to France had already separated them—he married a cultivated and charming Frenchwoman, to whom he was really attached and stayed faithful. There were no children by either marriage.

As a young man Bolingbroke, who had charm and looks, was a lover of women and drink. He always threw himself passionately into everything he did, both in his private and public life. But he combined pleasure with work; according to Swift he had a great respect for the character of Petronius 'whom he would gladly be thought to resemble'. Even without the excitement of politics he was able to work as a scholar and writer; long periods in his life were spent in this way, especially in his enforced retreats; his reading was wide, his memory firm, his taste good, his intelligence not profound, but practical and clear. Although his own literary talent was less creative than expository, he dominated—in character as well as rank—a circle of wits. Pope and Swift knew him intimately and remained his close friends. His correspondence with them, though sometimes affected, has many fresh and human touches; his conversation steered happily *'from grave to gay, from lively to severe;/ correct with spirit, eloquent with ease,/ intent to reason, or polite to please'*. This is Pope's tribute, from the *Essay on Man* which was dedicated to him.

Statesman, orator, writer, scholar, wit, rake, this versatile man was also a sportsman who piqued himself on knowing his hounds by name and liked living in the country. He took country houses, both in England and France, and lived in them like a lord until he finally came back to die at Battersea. It is a mystery how his finances survived his extravagance; but he was seldom charged with personal corruption. He was warm in friendship and good to his relatives and to his friends; but he expected a lot from them in return and was quick to imagine slights. His life had more than its fair share of quarrels.

The picture that emerges is of a talented and fascinating man, strongly ambitious, highly self-centred, but capable of wide interests and warm affections. His temper was passionate, impetuous, disdaining hypocrisy and concealment. Both his intellect and his senses were keen; his main weakness was a lack of proportion; in spite of all his wit and gaiety he had little humour. He could control himself when he had set his heart on an object, but restraint was not natural to him; as a rule he was too ready to take offence, too impatient with what he had not initiated and too reluctant to bide his time. Feeling his superiority to most of his contemporaries he was spoilt by his early success and soured by his later failure; too much of his life was lived in capital letters or between inverted commas. Yet he was not a small man. He was at his most impressive when his energies and abilities were concentrated on some urgent piece of work. As Lord Stair said— and this could be his epitaph—he did not do things by halves.

The natural Bolingbroke is easily lost in the folds of the patrician drapery which his rank and taste supplied. It would be hard to find a man whose background inclinations and capacities were all so genuinely aristocratic. Bolingbroke had immense style; his manners were perfected in French and English society; his writing was based on classical models; he was a *grand seigneur* whether in the study or the drawing-room. It is possible to admire this aristocratic quality, but it is difficult to sympathize with anything so grand and thin, or to feel grateful to a person for embodying a tradition. If Bolingbroke has an appeal for the twentieth century it must be more in the passion and vigour which his manners could only partly school, or the flashes of imagination that quicken his ample periods.

His character helps to explain his career; so does the period in which he lived. His active political life was passed at a time of acute party conflict, mirroring a wider conflict between land and money, peace and war, partisans and opponents of the established church. Over all hung the question of the succession to the heirless queen. Until the succession was finally settled, and men knew where they stood, there was little scope for moderate courses. In his later life Bolingbroke admitted to having 'paid more than I owed to party' and never tired of depicting the evils of 'faction'.

St. John (as he then was) entered parliament as member for Wootton Bassett in time for the session which opened in February, 1701. He was in the Tory interest, attached himself to Harley and, three years later, was appointed Secretary-at-War at the age of twenty-six. In this office he won the friendship of Marlborough, whom he admired throughout his life. After two years in retirement he returned to office, with Harley, in 1710, this time in the more important post of Secretary of State for the Northern Department. Here he remained until the Queen's death in 1714, after which he never held office in England again. In 1712 he was created Viscount Bolingbroke, with no satisfaction to himself, since he had hoped for an earldom. At first distrusted by the Queen, because of his irregular life, he eventually replaced Harley (now Earl of Oxford) in her favour. But she did not live long enough for him to consolidate his position. As he wrote to Swift: 'The Earl of Oxford was removed on Tuesday, the Queen died on Sunday. What a world this is, and how does fortune banter us.'

He had two main preoccupations during the few years in which he held power. One was to secure the peace with France which the Tory squires were chief, but not alone, in demanding. He was personally responsible for most of the negotiations that ended in the Treaty of Utrecht. Charges of bad faith and underhand dealing can be brought and denied. It remains true that he worked, in conditions of great difficulty, with skill, vigour and patience; and that the conclusion was in the interest of this country. As peaces go, the Treaty of Utrecht was a good peace. The principle which it embodied (that of a

Portrait of Bolingbroke by a French artist,
in the National Portrait Gallery
(*see overleaf*)

Henry St. John
1678–1751
First elected to Parliament, 1701
Secretary-at-War, 1704–1708
Secretary of State, 1710–1714
Principal British negotiator of the
Treaty of Utrecht, 1713
Created Viscount Bolingbroke, 1712
In exile in France, 1715–1723
Secretary of State to the Pretender
July 1715–February 1716
Organized opposition to Walpole,
1725–1735

maritime, commercial, Britain only intervening in
Europe when the balance of power really demanded) was
consistent with what he later argued. Nor was his object
in working for this peace simply partisan or personal;
ambitious as he was he had enough of the statesman in
him to see what was at stake. As he wrote to Peter-
borough in 1712: '. . . a nice negotiation has been on foot,
wherein not Britain alone, but all Europe, not the present
age alone, but posterity are deeply concerned. . . .'²

Both as a statesman and writer Bolingbroke's chief
insight and surest touch were in foreign affairs. His aim at
home (his other main preoccupation when in power) was,
less impressively, to strengthen the hold of the Tory party
on the country. All for strong measures and against
compromise with the Whigs, he found himself increasingly at odds with the cautious and ambiguous Harley,
who was temperamentally so much his opposite. It is
possible to see in his conduct at this time a Straffordian
policy of 'thorough' on behalf of Church, Queen and
'the gentlemen of England'. Thus we find him writing
'What passed on Thursday in the House of Commons
will, I hope, show people abroad, as well as at home, that
no merit, no grandeur, no riches, can excuse or save any,
who sets himself up in opposition to the Queen.'³ We
find him promoting the much-criticized Schism Act of
1714, by which the education of Dissenters' children was
taken out of their parents' hands and entrusted to school-
masters licensed by the Bishops. We find him hoping that
the nation would elect 'honest country Gentlemen, who
will attend to the true interest of England'⁴ and that 'the
whole Church interest would, as one man, have laid hold
of this favourable conjuncture, to support the Queen,
exclusive of all other assistance, to vest all power in

themselves, and by these means to establish themselves for the present age and for futurity.'[5]

This seems the language of a high-flying Tory. It is not, as we shall see, the language of the later Bolingbroke, nor even of the young man of twenty who had described absolute Government as one of 'God's sharpest judgements'.[6] Nor, for that matter, is it the language of the Bolingbroke who, in 1713, gave a present to the actor Booth in Addison's *Cato* for 'defending the cause of liberty against a perpetual dictator'. Too much should not be read into Bolingbroke's domestic policy during the last years of the Queen's reign. Unlike his foreign policy it does little to illustrate or vindicate his principles. He always valued the throne, the Tory country gentlemen and—although a private free-thinker—the restraints of the established church; but his considered views on these matters were a good deal less extreme and emotional than the quotations in the last paragraph might suggest.

If 'thorough' was Bolingbroke's policy when in power, it was less for ideal than for practical reasons. Temperamentally he was always impatient of opposition; he was also single-minded in anything he did, so long as he was doing it; while he was in the Queen's service, he identified himself with it. His personal bent was actively re-enforced by party spirit. During Anne's last years party feeling, agitated by the questions of the peace and of the succession, was intense. In this struggle private interest played, quite openly, a massive part. Bolingbroke himself later admitted in the *Letter to Sir William Wyndham*:

'I am afraid that we came to court in the same dispositions as all parties have done; that the principal spring of our actions was to have the government of the state in our hands. . . .'

Politicians do not often see their private interest in conflict with the public good. Bolingbroke goes on to explain that the Tories ('We supposed the tory party to be the bulk of the landed interest, and to have no contrary influence blended into its composition.') thought of themselves as representing the real interest of the nation. Justified or not, it was party that counted. Anybody could see the dangers that threatened the Tories at the death of Anne. Bolingbroke seems to have aimed to establish the party so firmly that her successor would not be able to ignore its claims.

In the epitaph which he wrote himself Bolingbroke speaks of his 'attachment to Queen Anne'. It is useless to speculate how far this attachment was to the Queen's person, to the country, to the Tory party, or to himself. If his service to the Queen had been less wholehearted he might have been better placed after her death. But perhaps there was little he could have done to insure himself for the future except by strengthening his present hold. His strenuous efforts for the peace had not endeared him to Hanover. On the other hand there was little chance of a Stuart succession in defiance of the Act of Settlement, so long as James remained ostentatiously Catholic. There is some evidence of contact between Bolingbroke and the Pretender during Anne's reign, but none that need be taken very seriously. Most statesmen in his position would have thought it prudent to keep a line open to the court of St. Germain. It seems beyond doubt that there was no fixed design, in the mind of Bolingbroke or of the Tories as a whole, to alter the succession.

The tired Queen died, earlier than he could have hoped, and his game, whatever it was, was up. George came over and brought back the Whigs, thirsting for blood. A few months later Bolingbroke, fearing impeachment for high treason, fled to France. Would he have done better, like Oxford, to stand his ground? He might well have had a severer sentence than Oxford's two years in the Tower; there is nothing to show that his future career would have benefited. His reputation might have stood higher; but he was fitted for action, not martyrdom. He himself explained that he 'abhorred Oxford to that degree, that I could not bear to be joined with him in any case'.⁷ Nothing rings more true.

The decision to fly led a few months later to another decision, perhaps more difficult to defend. Bolingbroke entered the service of the Pretender as Secretary of State. Reports of growing Jacobitism in Great Britain, appeals from Tory friends and resentment at the prosecutions against him at Westminster, determined him on this step, which he afterwards bitterly regretted. Seven months later, as a result of the intrigues of others, some indiscretions of his own and an essential incompatability with his master, he was dismissed. He brought his usual ability and energy to an unlucky cause; the failure of the '15 was not his fault; Berwick acknowledged that he had done all he could. Once dismissed, he never flirted with Jacobitism again and, for the rest of his life, worked to rid the Tory party of its influence.

The rest of his career is bound to seem a decline, though it had its achievements. Having despaired of the Pretender he could only look to King George for political scope. It took seven years of good behaviour and the influence of his friends before the King pardoned him and he could return to England. In 1723 he visited London and discovered, after a brief interview with Walpole, that there was no chance of collaboration between them. It was not till 1725 that a Bill was passed enabling him to enjoy his family estates. Even then he was never allowed to take his seat in Parliament. As he wrote to Swift: '... the attainder is kept carefully and prudently in force, lest so corrupt a member should come again into the House of Lords and his bad leaven should sour that sweet, untainted mass.' He succeeded in obtaining one interview with George I, but it did not lead to anything. His hopes for power, though continually revived, gradually came to an end.

But he was not inactive during the twenty years or so of vigour that were left to him. By means of hospitality, personal influence and brilliant journalism (his celebrated writings in *The Craftsman*) he kept alive the idea of opposition to the comfortable Whig oligarchy of Walpole and his successors. He was continually engaged in inspiring, or in leading from behind the scenes, coalitions of Tories and dissatisfied Whigs. At times triumph seemed near. But even the fall of his chief enemy, Walpole, in 1742 was not followed by the creation of a coalition ministry. Bolingbroke's achievement during these years remained that of an opposition statesman or 'anti-Minister'. It was not an unimportant achievement. The later development of the parliamentary system in Great Britain probably owes more than is generally realized to Bolingbroke's attacks on Walpole's management. It is ironical that this should have been the main domestic contribution of a man who could not brook opposition himself and whose ideal was that of a benevolent and popular government representing a united nation.

Bolingbroke's career is hardly edifying; a friendly

biographer has to face successive shocks. Apart from his changes of course, he was not scrupulous in his choice of means; it seems fairly clear, for instance, that he was ready to accept French help and money at one moment during his opposition to Walpole. But his conduct should not be judged without some understanding of his character and predicament. It would have been difficult for an active man to have steered a straight course in the waters in which he found himself; and Bolingbroke was nothing if not active. If he was ambitious, arrogant and grandly theatrical, he was also able, enlightened and frank. He was capable of real energy, real feeling and real thought. Whatever his faults it will not do to dismiss him as a second-rate charlatan; his weakness was too much, rather than too little, passion. There is more weight in the charge that his career was not of a piece; that his motive was ambition not principle. But is this distraction between ambition and principle really such a valid one? Bolingbroke wanted power; when he had it he meant to use it in his own, necessarily enlightened, way. That is surely true of all great statesmen; none succeed, or wish to succeed, unless they are ambitious; none succeed permanently unless they identify themselves with some particular style of government, capable of giving some form and meaning to their actions. The style may help to inspire the ambition; but in turn the ambition creates the style. How many young men want to get to the top, and to leave their mark there, before they have settled their beliefs! Nor does a statesman's 'style' necessarily consist in a fixed set of principles. Some statesmen succeed in wedding their personalities to a set of principles which they never desert; others have equally strong principles, but feel the need to change them; others again seem to stand for little except themselves and their countries. Bolingbroke really belongs to the third class. He did indeed have principles; I have suggested that his use of power involved, in home affairs, some distortion of them. But he did not develop these principles properly until he was out of office—he was in it at a time of particular crisis and difficulty—and they would never have been a close guide to practical government.

None of this—whether the attack or the defence—is really relevant. In the last resort it is the weight and colour of a statesman's personality, not the purity of his principles or the uniformity of his conduct, that command respect. The dramatic growth and change of Gladstone's principles does not detract from his reputation as a serious statesman. If Bolingbroke commands less respect it is not so much through inconsistency or lack of principle (however Themistoclean his conduct he at least stood by his party connection), as because of the tendency to excess, the lack of control and proportion, so marked in his character. He could master these weaknesses when he had work to do; but he was denied a lasting opportunity or cause. Or perhaps, to put the matter more simply, it was failure that underlined his weaknesses and changes of course, when success would have redeemed them. He felt the reproach himself, however much he might try to present a marble front to the world. The fine language of his epitaph is really less convincing than the revealing letter[8] in which he wrote to Swift:

'Might not my life be entitled much more properly a what-d'ye-call-it than a farce? Some comedy, a great deal of tragedy, and the whole interspersed with scenes of Harlequin, Scaramouche, and Dr. Baloardo, the proto-type of your hero Oxford.'

Whatever his conduct Bolingbroke's principles, once he began to develop them in his writings, had the consistency I have already claimed for Disraeli's. He was justified in insisting in 1731: 'As far as I am able to recollect, my way of thinking has been uniform enough for more than twenty years. True it is, to my shame, that my way of acting has not been always conformable to my way of thinking. My own passions, and the passions and interests of other men still more, have led me aside . . . I have paid more than I owed to party, and as much at least as was due to friendship.'[9]

All Bolingbroke's political writings had a practical end in view. They were weapons in his political struggle and, in spite of their elegant style, should really be judged as tracts or superior journalism. At one moment he is defending, or explaining, his past conduct; at another he is attacking the foreign or domestic policy of the Walpole administration; at another he is trying to argue the Tories out of Divine Right and Jacobitism, or to lay the basis for a new 'national' government. These preoccupations do not prevent some able analysis of British and diplomatic history; but even such passages are seldom written with the detachment usually expected of an historian. Bolingbroke thought highly of history, but chiefly as a school for politicians. The proper end of historical study was, to his mind, 'a constant improvement in private and in public virtue'.[10] As usual, he is at his best in dealing with foreign affairs. The *Remarks on the History of England* show some real insight—for instance in emphasizing the rise of the bourgeoisie under the Tudors, the achievement of Elizabeth and the mistakes of the early Stuarts. But they serve too often as a cover for attacks on his living enemies. Historical analogy was a prudent and convenient weapon.

In writings of this kind it is inevitable that there should be some shifts of emphasis. The tone of the *Idea of a Patriot King* is more monarchical than that of the *Dissertation upon Parties*, which was meant to reconcile moderate Whigs and Tories rather than to influence the heir to the throne and his advisers. Nevertheless all these writings reflect the same basic political outlook. It is easily summarized, since Bolingbroke's views were neither subtle, mysterious, nor profound, and were always clearly, if rather amply, expressed.

Bolingbroke's message was, in brief, that the British constitution was as near perfect as possible, if it could be allowed to function properly, without distortion by King, Lords or Commons. It was happily suited to the genius and situation of the country. Liberty was its great object. To it 'we owe our riches, our strength, and all the advantages we boast of . . .' '. . . the greatest good of a people is their liberty.'[11] Liberty was to be achieved by a proper balance between the different classes and estates. The spirit of faction (throughout contrasted with the spirit of liberty) would of course always be ready to rear its ugly head. The chief guarantee against this lay in the crown. The Prince (who 'holds an office and owes a service')[12] must respect the rights of the different classes and rule by love and persuasion. A good prince, who respected the spirit of liberty, would be voluntarily supported by the nation. '. . . the peace and prosperity of a nation will always depend on uniting as far as possible, the heads, hearts and hands of the whole people.'[13] He should work closely with a free parliament, elected without corruption and not packed by hired supporters of the administration.

Bolingbroke throughout regarded the landed interest

as the backbone of the nation. He wrote in his last work: 'The landed men are the true owners of our political vessel: the moneyed men, as such, are no more than passengers in it.'[14] He had pleaded in support of the Landed Property Qualification Bill, in 1711, that 'we might see a time when the moneyed men might bid fair to keep out of that house (the House of Commons) all the landed men.'[15] But, in spite of this prejudice against the Whig financiers, he was very much alive to the value of trade to Great Britain. He wanted to suppress the standing army and develop the fleet and the colonies. His vision of a maritime, insular, colonial Britain, was Periclean. The great value of the union with Scotland had been (he argued) that it enabled the country to exploit the advantage of its insular position: 'an advantage which, constantly attended to and wisely improved, would place the British nation in such circumstances of happiness and glory as the greatest empires could never boast.'[16] With the continent Great Britain should play the part of a good neighbour and fair trader, only intervening in continental affairs when her interests, or the balance of power, absolutely required—and then in effective strength.

There is not much in Bolingbroke's political writings about his attitude towards the church. Though sceptical of miracles and intolerant of priestly government, he was not an atheist; he believed in natural, if not in revealed, religion. The last words that Chesterfield heard Bolingbroke say were: 'God who placed me here will do what He pleases with me hereafter; and He knows best what to do. May He bless you!' But his views were certainly not those of a good member of the Church of England. There has been much criticism by historians of Bolingbroke's championship of Church interests as a Tory leader and particularly of his promotion of the Schism Act,* which seemed to McCarthy to be 'an act of religious persecution, fitted only to be the work of the stupidest bigotry'. Bolingbroke later excused and apologized for the Schism Act as a party measure. But his private views were quite compatible with a belief in the value of the established church as an institution making for political unity and stability. He wrote to Swift that he detested the character of *esprit fort*; such men were 'the pests of society, because their endeavours are directed to loosen the bonds of it, and to take at least one curb out of the mouth of that wild beast man, when it would be well if he was checked by half a score others.'[17] Qualified persons should use their reason freely and impartially; but they should 'think for themselves and to themselves' without disturbing the peace of the world. In the Introduction to the *Letters or Essays addressed to Alexander Pope* he maintained that 'things evidently false might deserve an outward respect, when they are interwoven into a system of government'; and again: 'I neither expect nor desire to see any public revision made of the present system of Christianity. I should fear an attempt to alter the established religion as much as they who have the most bigot attachment to it, and for reasons as good as theirs, tho not entirely the same. I speak only of the duty of every private man to examine for himself. . . .'

It is easier to reconcile this point of view with Bolingbroke's political conduct than with the posthumous publication of his writings on religion. There are in any

* see page 49

case obvious weaknesses in a philosophy which enjoins private scepticism together with public acquiescence. But Bolingbroke must have compared his attitude with that of a cultivated Roman under the Empire, publicly observing the rites of the state religion yet in private completely aloof from it. Bolingbroke was steeped in the classics; they help to explain much of his political, as well as his philosophical, thought. The importance he attached to the constitution, with its balance of democratic, aristocratic and monarchical elements, is entirely in the classical tradition. His attacks on the Walpole system are strongly reminiscent of the Roman historians of the early Empire, particularly of Tacitus, who was a 'favourite author'.[18] They are redolent with the same feeling of doom, the same sarcastic indignation, the same sense of exile from power and the same fear for present—and respect for past—public virtue.[19]

The publisher's preface to the 1777 Edition of Bolingbroke's Works claimed: 'Whatever may have been the decision of the publick, concerning the philosophical works of Lord Bolingbroke, it is universally agreed, that his political writings contain a perfect system of practical politicks, written with an energy of style, and a strength of reasoning, not to be found in the essays of our most celebrated writers upon government.' This is as flattering as most publisher's blurbs. But, if it exaggerates the merit of Bolingbroke's political writings, Burke's criticism, quoted at the head of this chapter, is certainly too severe. Burke was prejudiced by his philosophical differences with Bolingbroke; he had written the *Vindication of Natural Society* in 1756 as a satirical attempt to show that Bolingbroke's arguments in favour of natural religion could also be advanced in favour of natural society.

Bolingbroke's writings have not the depth of Burke's; but they have clarity, elegance and common sense. His tendency to 'ramble too long in generals'[20] is redeemed by his skill in expounding party and diplomatic history, by the freshness of his judgements and by his pithy and imaginative phrases. He writes like the orator he was, with all the 'flowing happiness of diction' that Chesterfield said was habitual to him. Sometimes there is too much flow, but it never lacks vigour; sometimes there is too much affectation, but at least it keeps clear of cant.

In some ways Bolingbroke's 'generals', or central ideas, are the least interesting part of his writings. My summary of them is perhaps over-simplified, but any account would show them to be simple. They may not be superficial, but they sometimes seem facile. This is partly the effect of Bolingbroke's clear and flowing style, which tends to disguise the originality of much of what he had to say. Although he owed a great deal to Locke, and no doubt to other sources, he certainly thought for himself; his writings must have made much more vivid an impact at the time than they can possibly do now. De Lolme's and Blackstone's constitutional writings appeared well after Bolingbroke's death. Montesquieu was in England from 1729 to 1731; but his *De l'esprit des Lois*, with its flattering analysis of the free British constitution, was not published till 1748. The *Dissertation upon Parties* preceded Hume's essay *Of Parties*, which came out in 1742.

It is easy to criticize Bolingbroke's vision of a free, balanced and united society as utopian and inadequate. In some ways his *Idea of a Patriot King* foreshadowed the reign of Victoria; but Victoria had much less direct power than his Patriot King would have had, and the party system (which he condemned in theory, though his practice encouraged) flourished in her reign as never before. He did not foresee how the party system was to develop; he was also blind, with his contemporaries, to the class struggles that were to come. Prescient as he was of Great Britain's maritime and colonial career, he had no special insight into economics and did not realize how much of the country's prosperity would be due to her 'moneyed interest'. Whatever justification there was for his vision of government lay more in the past—in the reigns of Elizabeth and Henri IV of France—than in the future.

But something survives the criticism. Bolingbroke was writing for the early Georgian age. At that time the country had reached a rare, if temporary, social equilibrium and men were tired of the political and religious conflicts of the Stuart era. An able king, loving and loved by his people, could perhaps have realized something of Bolingbroke's ideal, without recourse to the systematic corruption practised by the governments of the day. Bolingbroke was right to argue that a good government can, and must, secure a free people's affections. The political lethargy under Walpole may have been a necessary phase in the country's evolution; but Bolingbroke helped to keep alive a spirit that was to sustain his countrymen under the two Pitts, in the Seven Years' and Napoleonic Wars.

This is not simply a flight of fancy. Bolingbroke knew the elder Pitt and had a regard for him; in return Pitt read Bolingbroke's writings and, at least at one period, admired him. Bolingbroke also had close connections with the circle of the future George III and his father, Frederick. Baratier refers to a memorandum of December 1752, in which various gentlemen complained that the education of the prince was confined to friends and pupils of the late Lord Bolingbroke. Whether or not George III had personally read, or digested, *The Idea of a Patriot King*, it was fully in keeping with its spirit that he came to the throne glorying in the name of Briton.

It would be beyond the scope of this essay to attempt a full picture of the extent to which Bolingbroke was influenced by, or himself influenced, others. Sichel suggests that he left his mark on Gibbon, who stayed in the house of his former secretary, Mallet, after going down from Magdalen. There was certainly a family link. In his autobiography Gibbon records Lord Bolingbroke's opinion of his grandfather (Mr. Edward Gibbon, a Commissioner of the Customs in the Tory administration of 1710–1714) that 'he never conversed with a man who more clearly understood the commerce and finances of England'. But this anecdote can hardly have been his only debt to Bolingbroke. Writing of his own early twenties, Gibbon says: 'The favourite companions of my leisure were our English writers since the Revolution: they breathe the spirit of reason and liberty; and they most seasonably contributed to restore the purity of my own language, which had been corrupted by the long use of a foreign idiom. By the judicious advice of Mr. Mallet, I was directed to the writings of Swift and Addison . . .' Gibbon goes on to pay a tribute to Robertson and Hume. He does not mention Bolingbroke; but it seems unlikely that Mallet did not also direct him to his writings, since (being the 'beggarly Scotchman' of Dr. Johnson's fulmination) he had edited them a few years before. At any rate Bolingbroke's oratorical style, shorn of some of its seventeenth-century gusto, but with a heightened polish and precision, seems to live on in Gibbon's periods. Immortality at second hand; but of a suitably monumental kind.

Photograph of Bolingbroke's monument
in Battersea Church
(*see overleaf*)

"Here lies Henry St. John
In the reign of Queen Anne
Secretary at War, Secretary of State and
Viscount Bolingbroke
In the days of King George I and King George II
Something more and better.
His attachment to Queen Anne
Exposed him to a long and severe persecution;
He bore it with firmness of mind.
The latter part of his time he spent at home
The enemy of no national party
The friend of no faction;
Distinguished under the cloud of a proscription
Never entirely taken off
By zeal to maintain the liberty
And restore the ancient prosperity
Of Great Britain.
He died the 12th December 1751
at the age of 73."

(This epitaph was composed by Bolingbroke
himself, together with the epitaph to his
second wife, which appears on the same monument.)

Chapter 4

BOLINGBROKE AND DISRAELI

The *Dictionary of National Biography* represents
Bolingbroke as advocating, in *The Idea of a
Patriot King*, 'a kind of democratic Toryism'. From the account in the last chapter,
Bolingbroke hardly emerges as a 'democratic Tory', any
more than as a dyed-in-the-wool legitimist. His position
is really that of an 'Old Whig'—that is to say, an admirer
of the Constitution as established—or restored—by the
Revolution of 1688, with its checks and balances and
distribution of power. His outlook is scarcely more Tory
than that of Burke, who described his own Whiggism
as consonant with that of the Whigs at the time of the
Revolution and under Queen Anne.

Bolingbroke believed in monarchy, but in a limited
one. So, of course, did Burke. So did that apostle of
Whiggism (whom Bolingbroke acknowledged as his
philosophical master), Locke. There is a passage in Locke's
Second Treatise of Civil Government which foreshadows
the theme of the *Patriot King* and Pope's '*Right divine of
Kings to govern well*':

'. . . he that will look into the history of England will

find that prerogative was always largest in the hands of our wisest and best princes, because the people, observing the whole tendency of their actions to the public good, contested not what was done without law to that end. . . .

'Such Godlike princes, indeed, had some title to arbitrary power by that argument that would prove absolute monarchy the best government, as that which God himself governs the universe by, because such kings partake of his wisdom and goodness.'

Bolingbroke's Toryism may be more evident in his attachment to the landed interest. But Swift held that 'the possessors of the soil are the best judges of what is for the advantage of the kingdom'.[1] And Swift, however Tory in church matters, seems otherwise to have favoured Old Whiggish principles. Disraeli described Lord George Bentinck, his partner in opposition to the repeal of the Corn Laws, as 'a Whig of 1688' who 'wished to see our society founded on a broad basis of civil and religious liberty'. But Lord George, again according to Disraeli, held 'our territorial constitution' to be 'the real security of our freedom'.

The Old Whigs were neither against the Monarchy nor the Land, though they may have been less wholeheartedly for them than the more ardent Tories. Nor were they against the Church. (With this in mind Swift contrasts the Irish Whigs under George I—'a sort of people, who seemed to think, that the principles of a Whig consisted in nothing else but damning the Church'[1]—with the English Whigs under Queen Anne.) Lord George Bentinck's attitude—he was 'for the established church, but for nothing more, and very repugnant to priestly domination'—seems typically Old Whiggish. He would not presumably have gone so far on behalf of the Church as did Bolingbroke and his friends when they were in power. But the 'Schism Act' was, more or less avowedly, introduced for party reasons. Bolingbroke was less of a churchman in his writings. There he was quite ready to have his own fling at 'priestly domination'.

Disraeli's Toryism was complex and personal. The recipe called for a liberal use of English herbs and oriental spices. The mixture combined Radical, Traditional, Fascist and Socialist flavourings; but it scarcely tasted Whig. Mr. Gladstone commented after Disraeli's death, that his most striking characteristic was 'the utter absence of any love of liberty'.[2] This was not quite fair (Disraeli cared for liberties if not for liberty); but it was not quite false. Bolingbroke, as an Old Whig should, certainly rated freedom higher.

Disraeli's vision of the throne was romantic, almost mystical. Bolingbroke may have become attached to Queen Anne and used some monarchical expressions when he was in her service. But on the whole he looked at the monarchy through plain glasses and was content with plain language when writing about it. 'I am not one of those oriental slaves,' he says at the beginning of *The Idea of a Patriot King*, 'who deem it unlawful presumption to look their kings in the face. . . .'

Disraeli had a genuinely democratic vein, in the sense that he regarded the welfare of 'the people', the improvement of working conditions, and good relations between classes, as questions of supreme importance. There is little to show that Bolingbroke was much concerned with these questions, though he of course cared for the general prosperity of the country and was ready to recommend in 1749 a reduction in 'such of the taxes . . . as bear hardest on the poor laborers . . .'[3]

Common-sense and charity apart, there was little that was noticeably democratic about Bolingbroke's outlook. His temper was aristocratic; he believed in an *élite*;[4] his contempt for 'the rabble'[5] (in which he would have included the bulk of his own class) could be guessed from his character if it had never been revealed.

These differences between the two men were of course due, to a great extent, to the differences between the periods in which they lived. The French and Industrial Revolutions had intervened. But that does not make the contrast less striking. Disraeli's view of society was coloured by the Romantic Movement in its various forms. Bolingbroke's clearer, and more mechanical, conceptions belong to an age of Wren architecture, Lockian philosophy and Newtonian physics. It would, as always, be wrong to over-simplify; Bolingbroke's approach was more historical than Locke's and, as a man of sentiment and passion, he was not likely to under-estimate their effect on affairs. He has a streak that could be called romantic. Equally Disraeli has a streak that could be called classical. But the dominant colours are opposed.

If we turn back to the passages from the *Vindication* and *Sybil* in which Disraeli praises Bolingbroke,* we find that they exaggerate his talents and achievements, real though these were. They also show some misunderstanding of his position. It was not so much the Tory party, as the nation as a whole, that Bolingbroke would have 'recur to the ancient principles of their connection'. There was considerably less distinction in his mind than in Disraeli's between 'a real royalty' and 'a chief magistracy'. Disraeli

* See pp. 29 to 31, 32 and 33

may have been justified in claiming an historic Tory title to deal with Parliamentary reform.[6] But Bolingbroke's opposition to the Septennial Act, or Tory measures for the purity of elections, were not inspired by a wish to popularize Parliament. They sprang rather from an 'Old Whiggish' concern to prevent the undue dependence of a corrupt Parliament on the Crown or its Ministers. Nor was Bolingbroke really an advocate of a 'permanent alliance' with France. He was indeed against unnecessary intrusion in the affairs of the continent and he must personally have passed for Francophile. But he acknowledged that France had been left too powerful by the Treaty of Utrecht and he would certainly not have ruled out future struggles with her. In any case his conception of foreign policy was classic: 'A wise prince, and a wise people, bear no regard to other states, except that which arises from the coincidence or repugnance of their several interests; and this regard must therefore vary, as these interests will do, in the perpetual fluctuation of human affairs.'[7]

The second passage from Disraeli's *Vindication of the English Constitution*, quoted at the head of Chapter 2, is revealing. Its opening sentence may be thought exaggerated, but is otherwise fair enough. But the three sentences that follow are pure myth. There is no evidence that St. John either 'recoiled from the Tory tenets' or was 'opposed to the Whigs from principle', or indeed that he saw much to choose between the two parties when he entered politics as a very young man. We do not know why he decided to throw in his lot with the Tories; perhaps he had more friends, or saw more scope for advancement, in their ranks. At any rate he was content to act with his friends, under Queen Anne, and later admitted that he had sacrificed too much to party spirit. His period of 'vigilant and meditative independence' belongs to the end, not to the outset of his career; the imputation of inconsistency could hardly have been brought against him before Anne's death. There is nothing to suggest that 'in the earlier years of his career he meditated over the formation of a new party'. He may have contrasted the interests of a Whig 'Junto' with those of the 'gentlemen of England'; but that was not quite the same as 'a choice between oligarchy and democracy'. Finally the later Bolingbroke would surely have considered that it was only after he had ceased to devote himself 'absolutely to his party' that he really 'embraced the national cause'.

In short Disraeli viewed Bolingbroke in terms of his own epoch and experience. This gave him an insight into his predecessor, but one that was bound to be misleading. His debt was as much imagined as real.

Was the debt real at all? What was there really in common between the aristocrat and the Jew, between the philosopher and the novelist, between the rake and the dandy, between the sportsman and the dreamer, between the man who acted when young and reflected when old and the man who had to wait for his old age to realize any part of the ideas of his youth?

At least there were some personal qualities in common: some likenesses of intellect and imagination; a sense of theatre; above all, ambition and the will to excel. Perhaps Bolingbroke's ascendancy over the young Disraeli was at bottom as much a question of style as of anything else. Style of working; style of living; style of writing. It was through his writings that Disraeli knew Bolingbroke; they influenced his literary style at least as much as his political thought. Newman retained some of Gibbon's impress, in spite of the worlds between them. Similarly the eighteenth century lingers on, if only as a faint or distorted echo, in Disraeli's elaborate prose. Even at their most exotic, his novels can recall an earlier school in an occasional cadence of dignified rhetoric or a recurring vein of courtly irony. Who was it who wrote that William III 'committed the fatal oversight of neglecting to conquer the nation'? Or the following passage:

'. . . the State is become, under ancient and known forms, a new and undefinable monster; composed of a king without monarchical splendor, a senate of nobles without aristocratical independency, and a senate of commons without democratical freedom . . .'? Bolingbroke is the author in both cases; but the style could scarcely be more Disraelian.

Then Disraeli meant to be a rather unorthodox sort of Tory and yet to dominate his party. That is exactly what Bolingbroke seemed to have achieved. If Bolingbroke had led the church party as a free-thinker, why should his own Jewish origins stand in the way? Bolingbroke had shown that the Tory squires would accept a man of wit and education as their leader. Moreover some of his writings about the Crown, and some of his actions in opposition to Walpole, could be conveniently invoked to support the popular—and later the monarchical—views that Disraeli wished to propagate.

This is enough to explain Disraeli's curious hero-worship. He had no living hero. The elder statesmen of his youth were not an inspiring lot. He was forced to reserve his affection and admiration for men like Lord George Bentinck whose position and character he could respect, but whom he knew to be his intellectual inferiors.

His romantic and idealizing temperament needed something more. Baulked of a living hero it found a dead one—all the better for being beyond the reach of familiarity and ridicule.

The explanation may be adequate. But it seems slight. Can Disraeli have been quite so mistaken in sensing an affinity in Bolingbroke's political thought? Was he completely misled in taking him as his master in Toryism? Are there passages in Bolingbroke's writings more in sympathy with Disraeli's way of thinking than a broad analysis of them would suggest? These questions must be carried forward to the next chapter.

Chapter 5

RESTORATISM

In the last chapter I have argued that Disraeli's political creed was really quite different from Bolingbroke's. He was certainly fascinated, and influenced, by Bolingbroke's personality, career and style. He admired the principles of Bolingbroke's foreign and commercial policy. Both men were much concerned with the place of the Crown in the British Constitution; both set special store by the landed interest. But Disraeli's conception of society was romantic where Bolingbroke's was classical; his view of the Crown was more exalted and mystical; his care for the welfare of the 'people' more pronounced. Though both men professed attachment to traditional liberties, these were more central to Bolingbroke's scheme of things than to Disraeli's. In short the whole colour of Disraeli's Toryism, at once paternal and popular, was different from that of Bolingbroke's 'Old Whig' outlook, though they had some shades in common.

What of the admitted links between the two men? I have already written of the personal sympathy between them (at least that of Disraeli for Bolingbroke, it might well not have been returned); it is clear that this sympathy

73

encouraged Disraeli to seek and stress doctrinal likenesses. But the link of party is at least as important. Whatever the differences in their outlook, or in their political thought, the two men belonged to, and led, the right-wing party in British politics. Does this party connection go some way to justify Disraeli's myth-making? Could it imply a little of the unity that there would be, for instance, between two members of the Church of England, however separate in time and in their views on ritual?

In a certain obvious sense the answer is 'yes'. Both men had to deal with a party predominantly landed (this helps to explain the emphasis both placed on the landed interest); each was a strong party-man warmly attached to his supporters, though conscious of his intellectual superiority to them; each, however broad his views, had now and then to show his hounds game. But this sort of resemblance does not go very deep. The real question is whether the right-wing party, which both men led, had itself preserved any essential continuity other than its dependence on land: nothing of course so definite as a Church, with its sacred writings and ceremonies, but some loosely identifiable tradition of thought.

One might distinguish four main ways in which statesmen proceed; they can adapt, conserve, create or restore. All four methods are of course open to all political parties, particularly the first, since adaptation, for one reason or another, is an inevitable and continual process of political life. As to the second, what I have called the 'right-wing party' in British politics is now known as the Conservative party. But it is not now, and has never been, its only business to conserve. In times of violent and excessive change conservatism may be heroic;

in times of deep prosperity or exhaustion it may be sensible. But nobody contests that some change is now and then inevitable; nor could any party live long that was simply and invariably committed to the *status quo*. It could certainly not hope, unless in moments of crisis, to attract men of ideas. This has in fact been understood by the right-wing party and there have even been occasions, as during Bolingbroke's opposition to Walpole, when the left-wing party has seemed the keener to conserve, the right-wing to reform.

What then is the basic difference between the right-wing and the left-wing parties? It has been usual to think of the latter as being in some sense more progressive and popular. But there have certainly been times when Tory policy was more 'popular' than Whig and Conservative policy than Liberal; there have also been times, as I have suggested, when the right-wing party was the more anxious to progress. These progressive moments have of course sometimes been tactical rather than strategic; a case of 'dishing the Whigs' or of *sauter pour mieux reculer*. But that is not the whole story.

Analyses of political labels are bound to be more or less arbitrary. The cries and slogans change too frequently and mean too many things; the situations are too complex and confused; the terms used are too charged with emotion. It is difficult to find, and it may be a mistake to seek, any essence or continuity in a party that does not subscribe to a written body of belief. But one generalization can perhaps be made about the right-wing party. If we look at it fairly, throughout its history, we recognize it less by any 'exclusive' or 'reactionary' character, than by a general tendency to place some kind of reliance on the past, whether recent or remote.

The left-wing party is necessarily the more creative of the two; it draws its strength from some ideal system of intellectual or emotional principles, which it tries to realize in practice. As successive systems become unfashionable, the left-wing party changes its direction and name. As often as not its former principles then find a home in the right-wing party, which seeks to conserve their proved advantages. Thus the Tories of Bolingbroke's day, except for the Jacobite irreconcilables, largely adopted Whig constitutional theory; similarly inter-war Conservatism inherited economic principles that were originally Liberal.[1] One might well suppose that the right-wing party was never able to create of its own accord, that its principles were invariably taken from tradition or from its actual or former opponents. If so, it would seem impossible to point to any body of consistent right-wing (Tory or Conservative) opinion, other than a general preference for the tried over the untried. The Tory 'apostolic succession' shrinks to a platitude or swells into a mystery.

Nevertheless devout researchers have sometimes claimed to detect over the centuries a continuous thread, now brighter, now more faded, of true Tory doctrine. This doctrine conceives a graded but united society, in which the landed interest has some kind of basic, and rather mysterious, importance; a society guided by an established, or at least national, church and governed by a more or less absolute ruler, with traditional mystique, through traditional usages and with a paternal care for the welfare of his poorer subjects. In foreign affairs such a society acts without preconceived ideas except that of furthering its own national, and usually traditional, interests. This is a rough, but I hope not unfair, summary of Toryism as it has sometimes been pictured, notably by Disraeli himself, one of its chief exponents. It is certainly not the sort of outlook that has always characterized members of the right-wing party. In spite of its champions' efforts, it is not even easy to establish a regular line of Tory leaders who thought in this way. It becomes particularly difficult to do so in the early eighteenth century. We may go back to Laud and Strafford; but when we come to Bolingbroke, as I have suggested in earlier chapters, we are moving—in spite of the *Patriot King*, and in spite of his 'thorough' policy when in power—in a different political climate.

Whatever justification there may be for the view that this special brand of Toryism is the real contribution of the right-wing party to British political thought, is due, I think, to the party's constant preoccupation with the past. If one looks to the past of one's country for inspiration, rather than to abstract ideas, one is bound to see political events from a national and traditional point of view. The past achievements of the nation suggest a unity that current conflicts may obscure. The earliest and most stable elements in the national life—such as the Crown and the Land—come to seem specially important.

To some extent, therefore, this 'pure' or 'ideal' Tory doctrine is natural to the right-wing party and is not 'created' in the sense that Liberal and Socialist principles have been by their authors. But, unless there is an element of creation, its outline must be extremely vague, the ancestral voices heavily muffled. The power of the sovereign is, for instance, historically balanced by the traditional liberties of his subjects; how is the past to teach where the one begins and the other ends? It seems more logical to regard this body of doctrine as a theory of government in its own right—on a par with Socialism or Manchester Liberalism—which happens to have always roosted in the right wing, because it has found the historical atmosphere there comfortable. This has been easy for it to do, because in Great Britain this school of thought has normally been coloured, and tempered, by a reverence for tradition. Thus what could well become a revolutionary creed of absolute or totalitarian government (as it seems to have become in some other countries) has been able to wear a respectably conservative dress and to avoid looking too new.[2]

The extreme right in some countries appears as far removed from the moderate right as from the left—perhaps even farther. In what does its 'rightness' consist? Not in conservatism (which usually belongs more obviously to the middle), but rather in a fierce preoccupation with national destiny as opposed to cosmopolitan ideas. This 'national' approach to politics is certainly a general characteristic of the right wing, with its regard for the past. But, when pushed to extreme in Fascist theories of government, it becomes itself an idea rather than an instinct; it loses its nourishment from the national past and, with it, the invulnerability of a party that has no preconceived ideas except its attachment to ancestral achievements.

I conclude that 'ideal' Toryism, as soon as it becomes a practical and 'creative' guide to current politics, is little more the essential and invariable property of the right-wing party, than are opposing theories of government. This conclusion confirms the suspicion that, while the right-wing party frequently adapts and sometimes conserves, it can never create except from the blue-prints of past or present opponents, or of more or less accidental supporters. When it does create in this way it does so either for purely tactical advantage, or because it has been penetrated by alien ideas, or because the alien ideas of a previous generation have been digested and become a part of the national life. It can never, as it were, create from its own being, since otherwise it would have some creative principle to put before its devotion to the past—and this could not be permanent. The party would lose its only continuing identity. Creative principles, political systems, come and go; but there is always some kind of past to fall back upon.

If this survey is at all accurate it is hard to see how their leadership of so colourless, or so variously coloured, a party can provide the link between Disraeli and Bolingbroke for which we have been looking. It is of course true that it has always been a large part of the party's business to conserve; but, in a way, both Disraeli and Bolingbroke were reformers before they were conservers. However, there remains the fourth method of statesmanship to consider. By using this, the right-wing party can still reform, even though it is unable—for lack of fresh abstract ideas of its own—to create. Its preoccupation with the past can lead it to restore, as well as to conserve; and restoration is a kind of reform.

Restoration may be a reasonably well-defined and concrete process, as when the Stuarts and the Bourbons were returned to their thrones. But it is seldom that politics allow so precise an attempt to put the clock back to some loved and regretted hour. If I claim that both Disraeli and Bolingbroke were restorers, and that this was the most significant bond between them as political thinkers, I have in mind something more general, more akin to religious revivalism. Neither Disraeli nor Bolingbroke sought to return to an earlier age; they wanted to revive the political faith and conduct of their own times with what they held to be the spirit and manners of previous periods. They wanted a return to 'the old good-nature of the people of England'—a phrase of Lord Clarendon's which they both quoted. They might have been following Burke's famous advice:

'If the last generations of your country appeared without much lustre in your eyes, you might have passed them by, and derived your claims from a more early race of ancestors. Under a pious predilection for those ancestors, your imaginations would have realized in them a standard of virtue and wisdom, beyond the vulgar practice of the hour; and you would have risen with the example to whose imitation you aspired.'

A nostalgia of this kind may be to the Garden of Eden, the Golden Age, the State of Nature, or—less mythically —to political life seen in patriarchal or Happy Family terms. In *The Idea of a Patriot King* Bolingbroke describes 'the true image of a free people, governed by a Patriot King' as 'that of a patriarchal family, where the head and all the members are united by one common interest and animated by one common spirit'. In Pope's *Essay on Man* (which was dedicated to Bolingbroke and written under his influence)* the State of Nature is identified with 'the reign of God' and, after it has been corrupted by tyranny and superstition, the archetype of the restorer is given a central role:

" *'Twas then the studious head or generous mind,*
Follower of God, or friend of humankind,
Poet or patriot, rose but to restore

* But see Appendix

The faith and moral Nature gave before;
Relum'd her ancient light, not kindled new,
If not God's image, yet his shadow drew . . .'

But such visions may be too remote and Utopian to carry
weight in practical politics. Men need to be persuaded, if
they are to make a 'revivalist' or 'restoratist' effort, that
things were ordered better at some recognizable period in
their pasts. I shall try to show what periods attracted
Disraeli and Bolingbroke. If the result seems a little
absurd, it is worth bearing in mind that, for the restorer
himself, the emotional urge to heal and restore may be
more important than the actual characteristics of the
periods he seeks to revive. When he has concrete reforms
to propose, the past may provide an inspiration and
pretext rather than a practical guide.

Disraeli's mind might have taken a creative or speculative turn, but for the accidents of nineteenth-century politics, his historical bent and his sense of race. Even as it was,
his wish to restore past felicities sometimes looks more
like an attempt to create new ones. His interpretation of
the past is often so very highly-coloured and imaginative
that one wonders whether he is not using it purely for
propaganda purposes of his own—seeing the past in terms
of the present, instead of the present in terms of the past.
In 1870 he wrote that he had urged the reconstructed
Tory Party to achieve its objects '. . . rather by the use of
ancient forms and the restoration of the past than by
political revolutions founded on abstract ideas . . .'[3] But
was this advice really derived from a careful study of past
history?

Nothing in the products of Disraeli's subtle mind, at
once imaginative, ironical and realist, can be taken

confidently at face value. But, in a sense, face value is often the only value there is. Disraeli is not so much deep as complex. His goods, in all their various glitter, are displayed in his shop window, not kept darkly out of sight. It is not really his way (though it sometimes seems it) to practise conscious mystification of his audience for some inner, and concealed, purpose; on the contrary he is usually open and often surprisingly indiscreet. Even at his most mysterious, he is not trying to hoodwink; the mystery arises because he has to express ideas apprehended intuitively rather than logically. Besides working intuitively his mind moves on different levels; he is quite capable of finding the same idea at once genuinely impressive and genuinely ridiculous. It would not be in his nature to re-write history consciously; but he might well be content to draw superficial lessons from it, which would at the same time excite and amuse him.

My own guess is that Disraeli always realized with a part of himself, and with more of himself as he got older, that his interpretation of the past was romantic and, up to a point, shallow. But that is not to say that the interpretation was consciously intended to mislead. Moreover, however true or false, Disraeli learned something from it himself. It helped to shape his political ideas, just as these ideas helped to shape the interpretation. He was at once seeing the past and the present in terms of the other.

Apart from the particular lessons that he learned from history Disraeli was always able to find a general inspiration, sincere if vague, in the national past. To quote from a speech at Bingley in 1844: 'We are on the eve of a great change, which will bring back some of those old feelings, some of those ancient hereditary sentiments of loyalty and good faith and mutual trust, that once made

England great, and which, in my opinion, alone can keep England great.'

Here is the genuine revivalist or 'restoratist' note. It is often sounded by Bolingbroke in passages which (for he was an emotional man but a persuasive or impressive, rather than a moving, writer) touch more than most of his writings. Compare, for instance, his claim on his epitaph that he had been, during the latter part of his time, 'the enemy of no national party, the friend of no faction; distinguished under the cloud of a proscription never entirely taken off, by zeal to maintain the liberty and restore the ancient prosperity of Great Britain'. Compare also the passage in the *Remarks on the History of England* when he writes of 'a revival of the true old English spirit, which prevailed in the days of our fathers, and which must always be national, since it has no direction but to the national interest'.[4] Or the passage in the *Letters on the Study and Use of History*: 'When you look back three or four generations ago, you will see that the English were a plain, perhaps a rough, but a good-natured hospitable people, jealous of their liberties, and able as well as ready to defend them with their tongues, their pens and their swords. The restoration began to turn hospitality into luxury. . . .'[5] This was written in 1735-6. But Bolingbroke had already written to Sir W. Trumbull in 1698, before he was twenty: '. . . there was a time when *dulce et decorum est pro patria mori* was imprinted on our hearts, when zeal for liberty, courage, integrity and virtue were as much in fashion as the contrary vices are now. . . .'[6]

Other passages could be quoted from both writers to illustrate this general trend. But differences appear between them when the nostalgia comes to be more closely identified. Bolingbroke's nostalgia is chiefly to the reign

of Elizabeth. He is against the attempts by the Stuarts at
absolute government; and, in spite of his support for the
established church, he is against the tyrannical tendencies
which he attributes to the medieval priesthood (though he
admits that it 'was forced, on some few occasions, to be a
friend to the liberties of the people').[7] Elizabeth, in
shining contrast, 'was supported by the spirit of liberty;
and she overcame that of faction';[8] 'she united the great
body of the people in her and their common interest, she
inflamed them with one national spirit . . .'[9] Elizabeth, or
Henri IV of France, was Bolingbroke's model for his
Patriot King. But there is also an earlier nostalgia. The
increase in the wealth and power of the Commons, which
took place under the Tudors, brought us back 'in times
very distant and in circumstances very different, to the
principles of government, which had prevailed amongst
our Saxon ancestors, before they left Germany'.[10]

Bolingbroke's works contain frequent references to the
free constitution and 'spirit of liberty' of our Saxon
ancestors, with their 'Gothic institution of government'[11]
which had survived an 'almost continual struggle against
the usurpations of our princes, and the vices of our
people. . . .'[12] Swift, a strongly nostalgic restorer, who
celebrated the virtues of the 'English yeomen of the old
stamp' in *Gulliver's Travels*,[13] refers somewhere to the
wisdom of the 'Gothic institution' of annual parliaments.
This Gothic zeal was not confined to Tory circles. Bishop
Burnet records that the last thing he explained to Queen
Anne's son, the Duke of Gloucester, before his early
death, was 'the Gothic constitution . . .'.[14] But it had a
particular importance in Bolingbroke's scheme. It is
significant that he sees the Revolution of 1688 not as a
reform, but as a restoration, which 'renewed' the old

constitution, rather than altered it for the better, and 'brought it back to the first principles, and nearer to the primitive institution . . .'.[15]

Bolingbroke's admiration of things Saxon may be explained by the efforts of seventeenth century antiquarians.[16] It was shared by Disraeli, who made it a central theme of *Sybil*. The theme is indeed foreshadowed in *Coningsby*, where Mr. Millbank makes this arresting introduction:

'My only daughter, Mr. Coningsby, Edith: a Saxon name, for she is the daughter of a Saxon.'

In *Sybil*—where we are particularly concerned with the condition of the 'Saxon' lower classes—we learn that the civil liberties of the English had really depended on Saxon and Norman institutions rather than on Whig achievements. The young Queen comes to the throne with 'the blood and beauty of the Saxon. Will it be her proud destiny at length to . . . break the last links in the chain of Saxon thraldom?' Sybil is found reading Saxon reminiscences to her father. (Incidentally Sybil is an especially enthusiastic restorer. She remembers 'what this English people once was; the truest, the freest, and the bravest, the best-natured and the best-looking, the happiest and most religious race upon the surface of this globe . . .' and it is 'with a kind of sigh' that she says: 'But then Stephen does not want to recall the past . . . he wishes to create the future.') Even the clergyman, Mr. St. Lys, who is 'a younger son of the most ancient Norman family in England' is 'distinguished by that beauty of the noble English blood, of which in these days few types remain; the Norman tempered by the Saxon . . .'[17]

But once we take leave of our Saxon ancestors, with their Gothic institutions, we find some differences between Disraeli and Bolingbroke. The latter's approach to the past was more sober, less mystical and less entertaining. His values, too, were different. Disraeli's admiration for Elizabeth seems to have been less pronounced than Bolingbroke's; his sympathy for the medieval church was much greater. This was so even at the time of the *Vindication* (1835), when Disraeli appears to have been most under the influence of Bolingbroke—and also of Burke—and was most insistent on the preservation of traditional liberties. By the time he had come to Young England and the Trilogy of *Coningsby*, *Sybil* and *Tancred*, he had acquired an additional nostalgia—for the reign of Charles I. Bolingbroke, in spite, or because, of his dealings with the Pretender, showed little sympathy with the Stuarts in his writings. But in *Sybil* Charles I is 'a virtuous and able monarch' who laid down 'his heroic life for . . . the cause of the Church and the cause of the Poor'. In *Coningsby* the benevolent young landowner, Eustace Lyle, comes from 'an old Cavalier family', just as Waldershare in *Endymion* 'had some Stuart blood in his veins'.

Not that Disraeli was personally responsible for this Stuart enthusiasm; it was in the air of the age, of the Young England and Oxford movements. He liked to fancy that he had restored his country house, Hughenden Manor, 'to what it was before the Civil War'. But when he came to write *Endymion* in 1880 his reminiscences of Stuartomania were detached and affectionately ironical. Waldershare (George Smythe) is made to say: 'One never sees a pottle of strawberries now. I believe they went out, like all good things, with the Stuarts.' John Hampden, the leader of the High Church party in the Oxford Union, 'had portraits of Laud and Strafford over his mantelpiece, and embossed in golden letters on a purple ground the magical word 'THOROUGH'.'[18]

What does all this restoring enthusiasm amount to? Not much perhaps in the way of tangible results; though the development of the monarchy under George III and Victoria may have owed something to Bolingbroke's vision of Elizabeth, the development of Conservative social policy to Disraeli's vision of Charles I and the medieval church. But restoratist efforts should not be viewed simply in such terms. In *The Idea of a Patriot King* Bolingbroke writes grandly of the need to 'reinfuse the spirit of liberty, to reform the morals, and to raise the sentiments of a people'. He and Disraeli both helped to influence the general tone of the societies in which they lived. Disraeli's efforts may have been more successful; but he owed much to his predecessor, whether he read him right or not. Both men reminded their contemporaries that society was organic as well as mechanical. Thus Bolingbroke to Viscount Polwarth in 1739: 'Let the object of our conduct be determined by knowledge, by experience and reflection; let prudence regulate the measure of it, but let the sentiments of the heart animate the whole. I saw and I felt with great pleasure, that they animated yours, in an age and country where the fewest symptoms of them appear, and where the greatest want of them exists.' Thus Disraeli in a speech in 1844: 'The fact is, gentlemen, that society, like man, has a heart, and that is a truth which, for the last fifty years, seems to have escaped the consciousness of our rulers.' Finally both men worked to revive the spirits, and restore the fortunes, of their party and enabled it to survive into changed times. By their speeches and writings they attracted, and can still attract, imaginative minds to their support; by the device of 'restoratism' they reconciled conservatism with reform.

The 'device of 'restoratism'' cannot, under my definition, be a purely right-wing process. The past, even of one country, speaks with many voices. If a particular set of institutions are to be restored, or a particular spirit revived, they must be selected on some external principle. Bolingbroke, with his free Saxon institutions, and Disraeli, with his Stuart martyr, chose these periods because they suited their 'Old Whig' or 'Ideal Tory' views. These views may have been shaped, but they cannot have been created, by a study of the past. It could have suggested other, and quite different, lessons.

The romantic conservative, who takes pride in an old, and still flourishing, tradition is more completely at home in the right-wing than the restorer. Some creation is admittedly involved in any exercise of imagination. The romantic conservative may see a silk purse where others see a sow's ear. But his enthusiasm is less obviously creative than that of the restorer, who cannot point to living glories, but must evoke dead ones. On the other hand the restorer's enthusiasm, kindled by past events, is less obviously creative than that of the speculative thinker with a new system to offer. The restorer's choice of ideals is limited by the various forms that the national evolution has produced—or can be plausibly represented as producing. Though always something of an outsider on the right wing, he is more usually found there than on the left. He is at least like his party in looking to the past for inspiration.

The questions with which I began might now be answered as follows:

Disraeli was right to take Bolingbroke seriously,

though he idealized and partly misread his career.

There were important differences between the political outlooks of the two men.

There were also some resemblances; but these are hardly striking enough to constitute a coherent and specifically Tory body of political doctrine.

Nevertheless there was a fundamental likeness: each of the two looked on the world with the eyes of a restorer. They both felt the emotional urge to create, through revival, a united and contented society; for this work they preferred traditional tools and models.

Their 'restoratist' methods implied a regard for the past, which is the only permanent characteristic of the right-wing party to which they both belonged. It is this regard for the past that has given the party a kind of unity and has invited attempts, which can never be fully successful, to trace an inherited body of right-wing beliefs.

But what is to be gained from this preoccupation with the past? What is the reason of its strange appeal for the restorer and the romantic conserver? Let them restore or conserve systems that they happen to like or that have turned out well in practice. That is the object of the practical conservative; his aims are straightforward and it is easy to agree or to disagree with him. But the restorer and the romantic conserver usually take up their position on less solid ground. If Disraeli is at all typical their approach to the past is more emotional than scientific; they seldom behave as if they were patiently seeking historic truth. They preach, they evoke, they exalt; but they rarely stop to analyse or to sift the historical evidence in support of their views.

They seem to turn to the past less for practical guidance than for a kind of mystical illumination.

If this is so, it is surely because the political thinker with a practical object in mind is necessarily something of a moralist. He wishes to bring about a certain state of things, to realize—as far as possible—an ideal form of society. To this end he paints an ideal picture: lifelike, he hopes, but like life at its most colourful. In the same way a poet may describe sensations less as he has actually felt them than as he believes he could have felt them if he had really been on form. (Emotion may be recollected in tranquillity, but does not lose in the telling.) The poet exaggerates in order to make experience seem more significant; the political moralist exaggerates in order to persuade people to behave as he thinks they could if they would. The political thinker, who draws his inspiration from the past, naturally makes his chosen period or tradition look its best: like a commissioned portrait painter he paints from the life, but glosses over the pimples. If he prefers to paint from the life rather than from the imagination—if he would rather refer to past events than to theoretical ideals—it is because he happens to be the type of artist who prefers the real to the abstract and cannot dispense with a model.

The past can serve as a source of practical lessons or of social ideals. But these are not the only ways of justifying the backward look. We are obviously formed to a great extent, whether we like it or not, by what our ancestors thought and did. Our inheritance conditions the temper of our minds, the pattern of our lives. We dare not dispense with these traditionary influences unless we are ready to commit ourselves whole-heartedly to some new system of values; otherwise we are lost, at the mercy of our own impulses and divided from each other. There may be times when discontent with the existing order is so widespread that a clean break must be attempted, a new system chosen and ruthlessly imposed. The break will never be quite complete; the new regime not only sets up its own traditions but revives such pre-revolutionary ones as suit its book. Even so, the cost of the change can only be heavy; things of great value, in the lives of individuals if not in the social order, perish; suffering on a large scale is inevitable. Where the change is less radical—one compares the French with the Russian revolutions—the suffering may be less and fewer precious things may be lost; but the unity and self-confidence of society will take long to recover.

This is not of course to suggest that traditions should automatically be preserved and change eschewed. Nor is it to claim any precedence for the traditionalist over the progressive. But, given a society that has any health, it seems worth while to go to great lengths to marry change with tradition, to select from the real or imagined past enough to ensure some continuity in the midst of up-heaval. It seems worth while, with Burke, to 'make the re-paration as nearly as possible in the style of the building'.

It is to the public good that the past should not be forgotten. Private happiness may want it remembered, so that the present can be viewed in its depth and perspect-ive. Seen in their historic scheme our actions may seem less trivial and our habits more dignified. Perhaps life needs to be extended into the past or the future, or into some supernatural dimension, if it is not to look too little. There will always be some who are diffident about the future and do not credit the supernatural, but draw a kind of strength from sensing their obedience to an inherited rhythm.

Appendix

BOLINGBROKE'S VIEWS
ON THE ORIGINS OF
POLITICAL SOCIETY

The account of Bolingbroke's political doctrine in Chapter 3 is drawn from his political writings. His 'metaphysical' writings contain little political philosophy. In some of his *Fragments or Minutes of Essays*, however, he sets himself to vindicate the existence of 'the law of nature'. In the course of this (Fragments X–XVI) he treats of the way in which political societies came into being. This is his main excursion into political philosophy in the academic sense of the term; most of his writings on politics, like those of Disraeli, were more concrete—the work of a politician, rather than a philosopher. His analysis in the *Fragments*, if a little lacking in philosophical rigour, is full of common-sense and written in his usual robust and graceful style. It confirms his position as an 'Old Whig' with an un-Whiggish historical sense.

In this analysis Bolingbroke allows himself to part company, respectfully but firmly, from Locke. He criticizes Locke's view, developed in *The second treatise of civil government*, that 'the beginning of politic society depends upon the consent of the individuals to join into and make one society'; that men, being born free, enter into political society by an 'original compact' under which they agree to surrender some, but not all, of their rights; and that this compact is kept in force by the tacit consent of their successors. Bolingbroke argues that there was no compact; that the origins of society lie in the family, that men were consequently always in society and that the differences between natural and political society are not greatly significant. 'Societies were begun by instinct and improved by experience.' Men are naturally sociable and never lived as complete individuals, in Hobbes' brutal State of Nature. Political societies started in various ways; families might unite to form communities against some external threat; conquest and the transmigration of surplus population were other causes.

Bolingbroke shows in these pages that he does not subscribe to every word in the *Essay on Man*, although he inspired its outlines. Writing to Pope (for the *Fragments* are addressed to him) he says: 'You poets have given beautiful descriptions of a golden age, with which you suppose that the world began . . . I do not believe that men were as good, any more than I believe that other animals were as tame, by nature, as you represent them to have been in the primaeval world. . . .' Men are naturally sociable but, once their personal needs are met in society, 'self-love', which encouraged their social impulses, begins to encourage their anti-social ones. '. . . natural sociability declines, and natural insociability commences.' This is why there is discord between societies. 'The great commonwealth of mankind, cannot be brought under one government, nor subsist without any.' Similarly, within each society, the predominance of the affections and passions over reason explains the 'unnatural manner' in which the law of nature may be executed.

I have written earlier of Bolingbroke's Old Whiggish regard for liberty. Real though this was, it was a modified version of the passion that inspired the great Whig and Liberal thinkers. He does indeed claim it as an undoubted truth that 'all men are born to be free'. But he thinks that Locke's notions on the natural equality and freedom of mankind were carried 'a little further than nature, and the reason of things, will allow'. Social should be distinguished from personal equality. Nature has certainly not determined the inequality found in society: that is artificial and man-made. But there is a striking personal inequality in the human species. Bolingbroke was not unconscious of his own superiority to the mass; this passage is reminiscent of his doctrine of an *élite*, sketched in the *Letter on the Spirit of Patriotism*, where he refers to 'the few, who are distinguished by nature so essentially from the herd of mankind, that, figure apart, they seem to be of another species . . .'.

These differences with Locke are revealing. They seem to reflect that emotional bias which Bolingbroke and Disraeli have in common. Bolingbroke sees the origin of political society, not in a compact of individuals, but in family life. It follows that men in society should behave as members of a family, rather than as individuals with natural rights to safeguard and contractual obligations to fulfil. The atmosphere becomes cosier, less calculating and less distinct. The good prince becomes a father-figure. We come back to the picture in *The Idea of a Patriot King* of 'a patriarchal family, where the head and all the members are united by one common interest and animated by one common spirit'.

Nevertheless, the influence of Locke is marked, even in these fragments. Like Locke, Bolingbroke believes that the first type of government probably tended to be monarchical, after the model established by the *pater-familias*. Equally he follows Locke whole-heartedly in his attack on 'that ridiculous writer Filmer'* who had defended the divine right of absolute monarchy by arguing 'that Adam was an absolute monarch by creation; that his right had descended to kings; that all other men are slaves by birth, and never had a right to choose either forms of government or governors'. He declares roundly, in words with an almost transatlantic ring:

'. . . tho we believe that monarchy was the first form of civil government, and that paternal government might lead men to it; yet may we believe very consistently, and we must believe unless we resolve to believe against fact and reason both, that this, like every other form of government is of human institution, established by the people, and for the people; and that no other majesty, since the word imposes so much, is inherent in it than that which belongs to the supreme power of every state, wherever that power is placed.'

And it is clear from Letter XVII of the *Dissertation upon Parties* that Bolingbroke also follows Locke in his justification of an ultimate right 'to appeal to heaven' and to revolt. In the last resort, Bolingbroke suggests, 'the whole nation' have the right to resist the supreme

---

* Sir Robert Filmer, in his celebrated book *Patriarcha*, published in 1680.

legislative power if its actions tend to the subversion of the constitution. Here as elsewhere Bolingbroke's reverence for, and sense of, history do not lead him to extreme Tory views.

NOTES

Chapter 1

1 See, e.g., Chapter V of *The Spirit of Whiggism* written in 1836.

2 Artisan Dwellings Act, Friendly Societies Act, Labour Laws, Factory Acts, Amendment of Education Act, Agricultural Holdings Act, Rivers Pollution Act, Public Health Act, etc. There seems no reason to belittle this useful legislation, even if its scope was extensive rather than deep. Though the Home Secretary, Sir R. Cross, was the Minister chiefly responsible, he had Disraeli's full backing.

3 'Lord John Manners—a Political and Literary Sketch comprising some account of the Young England Party and the Passing of the Factory Acts—by a non-elector'—London, 1872.

4 Sidonia's words in Chapter 14, Book II, of *Tancred*.

5 Chapter 24 of *Lord George Bentinck*.

6 Chapter 10, Book IV, of *Coningsby*.

7 Though he attributes, in Chapter 10, Book IV, of *Coningsby*, an undefined superiority to the Caucasian species, which he held to include—among others—Arabs, Saxons and Greeks.

8 Chapter 8, Book V, of *Tancred* provides a particularly good example:
'Tancred entered the temple, the last refuge of the Olympian mind. It was [the Hellenic] race that produced these inimitable forms, the idealized reflex of their own peculiar organization. Their principles of art, practised by a different race, do not produce the same results. Yet we shut our eyes to the great truth unto which all truths merge, and we call upon the Pict or the Sarmatian to produce the forms of Phidias and Praxiteles.'

Chapter 2

1 George Smythe felt this fascination too. In *Historic Fancies* (1844) he wrote of Bolingbroke: 'His memory is mostly associated with his light, and graceful, and gifted youth—the very idea and type of universal fascination.'

Chapter 3

1 'It is impossible to find lights and shades strong enough to paint the character of Lord Bolingbroke, who was a most mortifying instance of the violence of human passions, and of the weakness of the most improved and exalted human reason. His virtues and his vices, his reason and his passions, did not blend themselves by a gradation of tints, but formed a shining and sudden contrast.

'Here the darkest, there the most splendid colours, and both rendered more striking from their proximity. Impetuosity, excess, to almost extravagancy, characterized not only his passions, but even his senses. His youth was distinguished by all the tumult and storm of pleasures in which he licentiously triumphed, disdaining all decorum. His fine imagination was often heated and exhausted with his body in celebrating and almost deifying the prostitute of the night; and his convivial joys were pushed to all the extravagancy of frantic Bacchanals. These passions were never interrupted but by a stronger ambition. The former impaired both his constitution and his character; but the latter destroyed both his fortune and his reputation.

'He engaged young, and distinguished himself in business. His penetration was almost intuition and he adorned whatever subject he either spoke or wrote upon by the most splendid eloquence; not a studied or laboured eloquence, but by such a flowing happiness of diction, which (from care perhaps at first) was become so habitual to him, that even his most familiar conversation, if taken down in writing, would have borne the press, without the least correction, either as to method or style.

'He had noble and generous sentiments, rather than fixed,

reflected principles of good-nature and friendship; but they were more violent than lasting, and suddenly and often varied to their opposite extremes, with regard even to the same persons. He received the common attentions of civility as obligations, which he returned with interest; and resented with passion the little inadvertencies of human nature, which he repaid with interest too. Even a difference of opinion upon a philosophical subject would provoke, and prove him no practical philosopher at least.

'Notwithstanding the dissipation of his youth, and the tumultuous agitation of his middle age, he had an infinite fund of various and almost universal knowledge, which from the clearest and quickest conception, and the happiest memory that ever man was blessed with, he always carried about him. It was his pocket-money and he never had occasion to draw upon a book for any sum. He excelled more particularly in history, as his historical works plainly prove. The relative political and commercial interests of every country in Europe, particularly of his own, were better known to him than perhaps to any man in it; but how steadily he pursued the latter in his public conduct, his enemies of all parties and denominations tell with pleasure.

'He had a very handsome person, with a most engaging address in his air and manners; he had all the dignity and good-breeding which a man of quality should or can have and which so few, in this country at least, really have.

'Upon the whole of this extraordinary character, where good and ill were perpetually jostling each other, what can we say, but, alas! poor human nature!'

(From Lord Chesterfield's *Characters*. Vol. 2, p. 448 of the 1845 Edition. Chesterfield was a close friend of Bolingbroke's and a good likeness seems to emerge through the *chiaroscuro*).

2 Parke's *Correspondence*: Vol. 1, p. 489.

3 Quoted in Petrie's *Bolingbroke*, p. 310.

4 Letter to Shrewsbury, May 1713, from Parke's *Correspondence*.

5 Letter to Lord Chancellor of Ireland, May 1711, from Parke's *Correspondence*.

6 Letter to Sir W. Trumbull, May 1698, quoted in Petrie's *Bolingbroke*, p. 20.

7 *Letter to Sir William Wyndham*. Works, Vol. 1, pp. 33–4.

8 Letter of August 30, 1729.

9 Letter to Swift of August 2, 1731.

10 Letter II *on the Study and Use of History.* Works, Vol. 2, p. 266.

11a Letter XII of *a Dissertation on Parties.* Works, Vol. 2, p. 166.

11b *The Idea of a Patriot King.* Works, Vol. 3, p. 66.

12 Letter XIV of *a Dissertation on Parties.* Works, Vol. 2, p. 188.

13 Dedication of *a Dissertation on Parties.* Works, Vol. 2, p. 13.

14 *Some Reflections on the Present State on the Nation.* Works, Vol. 3, p. 174.

cf. *A letter to Sir William Wyndham.* Works, Vol. 1, pp. 9–11.

15 From the Wentworth pp. quoted in Trevelyan's *The Peace and the Protestant Succession.*

16 *Remarks on the History of England.* Letter XVI. Works, Vol. 1, pp. 430–1.

17 Letter to Swift of September 12, 1724.

18 Letter V *on the Study and Use of History.* Works, Vol. 2, p. 341.

19 In a letter of 1740 Bolingbroke quotes Livy:
'*Ad haec tempora, quibus nec vitia nostra, nec remedia pati possumus, perventum est.*' But it is fair to add that he is usually more forward-looking than his classical models.

20 Letter X of *a Dissertation on Parties.* Works, Vol. 2, p. 134.

Chapter 4

1 Letter to Pope of January 10, 1721–22.

2 Magnus' *Gladstone,* p. 281.

3 *Some Reflections on the Present State of the Nation.* Works, Vol. 3, pp. 171–2.

4 This is the opening theme of the *Letter on the Spirit of Patriotism.*

5 See Bolingbroke's letter to Swift of July 21, 1721:
'Is it possible that one of your age and profession should be ignorant, that this monstrous beast has passions to be moved, but no reason to be appealed to, and that plain truth will influence half a score men at most in a nation, or an age, while mystery will lead millions by the nose?'

6 See Sichel's *Bolingbroke and his Times*, Vol. 1, pp. 244-7.

7 *Some Reflections on the Present State of the Nation*. Works, Vol. 3, p. 179.

Chapter 5

1 This is not a reference to Free Trade (Imperial Preference could give the lie; in any case Bolingbroke, Pitt and Huskisson could be claimed as Free Traders, though not dogmatic ones), but to the assumption then current, which had not been part of earlier Tory doctrine, that measures for social welfare should not be allowed to interfere with the laws of supply and demand.

2 The 'imperialist' phase in British right-wing policy, at the end of the nineteenth century, shows the influence of this doctrine, in external affairs, at its height. Not that 'pure' Toryism need necessarily involve expansion. The parallel is not of course exact: but in fifth-century Athens it was the landowning conservative opposition that resisted the city's imperialism. Perhaps, if a 'pure' Tory feels confident enough to proselytize, he expands. Otherwise he fears contamination, draws in his horns and tends to become a 'little Englander'.

3 From the General Preface to the Hughenden edition of the Novels.

4 Works, Vol. 1, p. 277.

5 Works, Vol. 2, pp. 500-1.

6 Quoted in Petrie's *Bolingbroke*, p. 21.

7 *Remarks on the History of England*. Letter IV. Works, Vol. 1, p. 319.

8 Ditto. Letter XVI. Works, Vol. 1, p. 437.

9 *The Idea of a Patriot King*. Works, Vol. 3, p. 100.

10 *Remarks on the History of England*. Letter XII. Works, Vol. 1, p. 384.

11 See, e.g., Letter XVI of *a Dissertation on Parties*.

12 Ditto. Letter IX. Works, Vol. 2, p. 124.

13 In Glubbdubdrib Gulliver 'descended so low as to desire that some English yeomen of the old stamp, might be summoned to appear; once so famous for the simplicity of their manners, diet, and dress; for justice in their dealings; for their true spirit of liberty; for

their valour and love of their country. Neither could I be wholly unmoved after comparing the living with the dead, when I considered how all these pure native virtues were prostituted for a piece of money by their grandchildren.'

14 Vol. 2, p. 246, of the folio edition of Bishop Burnet's *History of his own Times.*

15 Letter IX of *a Dissertation on Parties.* Works, Vol. 2, p. 123.

16 See Wedgwood's *The King's Peace*, p. 433.

17 According to Buckle, Mr. St. Lys was drawn from the Rev. F. W. (afterwards Father) Faber, who was addressed by George Smythe in a sonnet as 'Dear Master'. If so, it was Disraeli's imagination that supplied his ancestry. But all Disraeli's heroes have ancient lineage, of one kind or another, and most of them—an infallible sign of breeding in his novels—short upper lips.

18 A whole passage from Chapter XL of *Endymion*, in which the elderly Disraeli gently satirizes the enthusiasms he had once helped to propagate, is worth quoting. Waldershare is a devout, if erratic, believer in the Tory 'apostolic succession'. The scene is set in the home of the Rodney family in Warwick Street:

'Occasionally there was only conversation, that is to say, Waldershare held forth, dilating on some wondrous theme, full of historical anecdote, and dazzling paradox, and happy phrase. All listened with interest, even those who did not understand him. Much of his talk was addressed really to Beaumaris, whose mind he was forming, as well as that of Imogene. Beaumaris was a hereditary Whig, but had not personally committed himself, and the ambition of Waldershare was to transform him not only into a Tory, but one of the old rock, a real Jacobite. "Is not the Tory party", Waldershare would exclaim "a succession of heroic spirits, 'beautiful and swift,' ever in the van, and foremost of their age?—Hobbes and Bolingbroke, Hume and Adam Smith, Wyndham and Cobham, Pitt and Grenville, Canning and Huskisson?—Are not the principles of Toryism those popular rights which men like Shippen and Hynde Cotton flung in the face of an alien monarch and his mushroom aristocracy?—Place bills, triennial bills, opposition to standing armies, to peerage bills?—Are not the traditions of the Tory party the noblest pedigree in the world? Are not its illustrations that glorious martyrology, that opens with the name of Falkland and closes with the name of Canning?"

' "I believe it is all true", whispered Lord Beaumaris to Sylvia, who had really never heard of any of these gentlemen before, but looked most sweet and sympathetic.

' "He is a wonderful man—Mr. Waldershare," said Mr. Vigo to Rodney, "but I fear not practical".'

INDEX